CAREERS IN HEALTH LAW

LAWRENCE SINGER
MEGAN BESS
KRISTIN FINN

AMERICAN BAR ASSOCIATION
Health Law Section

Cover design by Monica Alejo/ABA Publishing.

Printed in the United States of America.

18 17 16 15 14 5 4 3 2 1

Library of Congress Cataloging-in-Publication Data

Singer, Lawrence E., author.
  Careers in health law / by Lawrence Singer, Megan Bess, Kristin Finn; Section of Health Law, American Bar Association.
     pages cm
  Includes index.
  ISBN 978-1-62722-713-1 (alk. paper)
  1. Health lawyers--United States. 2. Law--Vocational guidances--United States. I. Bess, Megan, author. II. Finn, Kristin, author. III. American Bar Association. Health Law Section, sponsoring body. IV. Title.
  KF299.M43S58 2014
  344.7303'21023--dc23
                                    2014027153

Discounts are available for books ordered in bulk. Special consideration is given to state bars, CLE programs, and other bar-related organizations. Inquire at Book Publishing, ABA Publishing, American Bar Association, 321 N. Clark Street, Chicago, Illinois 60654-7598.

www.ShopABA.org

Contents

About the Authors

Lawrence Singer (Author, Editor)

Larry Singer is the Director of the Beazley Institute for Health Law and Policy at Loyola University Chicago School of Law. He is also the Associate Dean of Distance Learning and an Associate Professor at Loyola. Larry's primary teaching and research focus is on transactional and regulatory matters, as well as access to care.

Larry was previously an attorney, and then partner, with the Chicago office of McDermott Will & Emery, where his practice focused on general corporate and transactional matters, medical staff affairs, and patient care issues. He also served as assistant to the general counsel of the American Hospital Association and as legal counsel in the America Hospital Association's Office of Legal and Regulatory Affairs. While there, Larry was one of the authors of an amicus curiae brief to the U.S. Supreme Court in the case of *Cruzan v. Missouri Department of Health.*

Larry has been recognized multiple times as a "super lawyer" in health law. He also has been inducted as a Fellow into the Institute of Medicine of Chicago. Larry has served on and chaired multiple boards, including those for a large regional health system, a facility for the developmentally disabled, and a local chapter of United Way. Larry received his Bachelor's degree, Master's degree, and Juris Doctor from the University of Michigan.

Megan Bess (Author, Editor)

Megan Bess is the Associate Director of the Beazley Institute for Health Law and Policy at Loyola University Chicago School of Law. She oversees all department operations, including strategic planning, development and implementation of student and academic policies, management of health law degree programs, externship placement and site relationships, marketing, and financial operations. Megan counsels and advises health law students on academic matters and career and externship placement in the health law field. Megan also teaches "Introduction to Legal Writing and Legal Study" for Loyola's online health law program.

Prior to working at Loyola, Megan was an associate attorney in the litigation group of Winston & Strawn. She earned her certification in mediation from the Center for Conflict Resolution in Chicago. Megan has served on the Youth Guidance Metro Board and on the board of the Chicago Chapter of the American Constitution Society. She volunteers with Rape Victim Advocates and at the East Lakeview Food Pantry. Megan received her Bachelor of Science degree from the University of Arizona and her Juris Doctor from Vanderbilt University Law School.

Kristin Finn (Author, Editor)

Kristin Finn is the Program Coordinator of the Beazley Institute for Health Law and Policy at Loyola University Chicago School of Law. Kristin works closely with the Director and Associate Director in overseeing the operations of the Institute. Kristin assists in student academic and career advising, budget management, and developing and coordinating Institute programming. Kristin is also the liaison between the Institute and adjunct faculty, the *Annals of Health Law* journal, and the Health Law Society. Kristin also teaches the course "Health Law Seminar Series" for Loyola's online health law program.

Prior to joining the Beazley Institute, Kristin received a Juris Doctor from Loyola University Chicago School of Law, where she was a Student Bar Association representative and an editor of the *Children's Legal Rights Journal*. Kristin also holds a Bachelor of Arts in Political Science from Saint Louis University.

Marianne Deagle (Contributor, Chapters 5 and 6)

Marianne Deagle is the Assistant Dean in the Office of Career Services at Loyola University Chicago School of Law. Marianne received her Bachelor's degree from the University of Michigan and her Juris Doctor from Washburn Law School. Following law school, Marianne worked for the Kansas Corporation Commission doing public utility regulatory law, and for the Department of Social and Rehabilitation Services doing health care policy. Immediately prior to joining Loyola, she was the Manager of Legal Recruiting at two large law firms.

Additional Contributors

The authors would like to extend their sincere thanks to those who helped with the research and editing of this book. Thanks to Ryan Meade, Jennifer Koltse, Kathryn Watson, Matthew Horton, Benjamin Van Gelderen, Anne Compton-Brown, Jessica Wolf, Jena Grady, Robert Hogan, April Schweitzer, Courtney Kahle, and Marlee Kutcher for your contributions. The authors would also like to thank the attorneys who contributed career profiles. Thanks to Amy Zimmerman, Colleen Burns, David Marx Jr., Doug Swill, Drew McCormick, Joe Monahan, John Steiner Jr., Kim Boike, Kyle Vasquez, Laura Morgan, Shawn Mathis, William Smart Jr., and Nancy Paridy.

Chapter 1

The Development of Health Law

Congratulations! You are considering a career in what we believe is the best area of legal practice.

How can we make this claim? In no other field than health law will you find the immediacy of policy and law that impacts every single human being, coupled with the most complicated regulatory and industry framework that exists in the United States. The health care industry encompasses services, pharmaceuticals, supplies, and equipment totaling almost 18 percent of the gross domestic product of the United States.

The practice of health law distinguishes itself from other areas of law by several factors. First, health law is a practice area organized around an industry, not a body of law. Thus, competent health lawyers need to have a thorough understanding of the health care industry, because as the industry changes, the laws and policies that impact health law change. This requires that health law attorneys understand the *business* of health care. Without knowing how health care works—how services and products are delivered and paid for—lawyers cannot provide adequate advice. Health care attorneys are routinely involved in strategic and business counseling with their clients, necessitating a keen understanding of the industry dynamics and key players involved.

Second, because of its organization around an industry, health law is in many ways one of the last remaining fields of general practice. Typical health lawyers have a knowledge base that includes many topics, such as bioethics, corporate, insurance, administrative, Medicare/Medicaid, tax, privacy, health information, and food and drug law. In addition, a number

1

of specialty areas within health law have arisen, including health law criminal law, antitrust, bankruptcy, life sciences, labor and employment, medical education, and many others. For attorneys entering the field, this diversity not only creates an exciting work environment, but it means that a multiplicity of skills are needed. There is no one "mold" for a successful health lawyer, but rather room for all interests and talents.

Third, health law is constantly changing. As the industry changes, so do the issues impacting the practice of health law. No health lawyer today is doing the same thing that he or she was doing one year ago, or even six months ago. The field is exceptionally dynamic, with clients constantly bringing new issues requiring legal advice to the fore. This environment of constant change can work to the advantage of attorneys who are new to the field—because certain areas of health law are new to everyone, it is possible for you to become an expert fairly quickly.

Fourth, health law practice is challenging. The stakes are big, sometimes literally life and death. Even in a corporate transaction, the impact of legal counseling can be significant. A new health care facility may be created, needed medical providers recruited to provide services for an underserved community, or an important pharmaceutical joint venture arrangement created. The fact that at the end of the day real people will be impacted by the work of health lawyers makes the practice of health law especially important and meaningful.

Fifth, health law is exceptionally entrepreneurial. As the head of any law firm would likely attest, the most entrepreneurial attorneys in the firm are the health lawyers. Health attorneys spend a significant amount of time keeping abreast of the field and sharing their knowledge with clients and colleagues through speeches, conferences, writings, and other means. Because the law and policy are continually changing, health lawyers become expert in identifying new areas of focus and reinventing their practice to respond to client needs.

Sixth, health lawyers are an exceptionally collegial bunch. While there are always exceptions, as a rule, attorneys who practice health law truly want to be in the field and understand that the health law bar (while numbering many thousands) is indeed a "small world." An ethos of respect and civility, indeed kindness, pervades the health law bar. This is especially true in the welcome extended to new attorneys entering the field.

Finally, the practice of health law is just plain fun. Yes, there will always be some difficult days in the practice of law. But, generally speaking, as a health care attorney you have the privilege of working on very important matters with highly sophisticated, intelligent clients who present interesting dilemmas and who genuinely appreciate your ability to wend your way through a myriad of complicated laws and industry practices to develop an approach that satisfies their needs. For an individual practicing law, it does not get much better than this.

Because the field is so large, and the options to work within the field so many, it is important to understand some of the key aspects of the health care industry. In the sections that follow, we will first review the key actors in the health care industry and then consider the major forces impacting the provision of health care. Next, we will review some of the key trends impacting health care. We hope that as you read these sections not only will you gain a basic understanding of some of the key aspects of health care, but you will also begin to identify potential areas of interest to you in focusing your career.

Health Care Industry Background

In the United States, total health care expenditures in 2010 were $2.6 trillion, with expenditures expected to climb to $4.6 trillion by 2020.[1] Almost 18 percent of the U.S. gross domestic product is spent on health care.[2] Clearly, health care is not an industry in decline!

It can be confusing, however, to consider the health care "industry" because it is comprised of so many different types of entities, from individual

---

1. CTRS. FOR MEDICARE & MEDICAID SERVS., *National Health Expenditure Projections 2010-2020–Forecast Summary*, https://www.cms.gov/Research-Statistics-Data-and-Systems/Statistics-Trends-and-Reports/NationalHealthExpendData/downloads/proj2010.pdf (last visited Mar. 25, 2014).

2. *Id.*

practitioners to suppliers of laundry services to multinational pharmaceutical companies. Because of this breadth and magnitude, the industry is typically segmented into four categories: providers, suppliers, payors, and pharmaceuticals. Although this segmentation is valid for purposes of understanding some of the unique issues faced by entities within the sector, it is important to understand that these sectors are continually interacting with each other and that often the lines are becoming blurred. Thus, for example, the provider side (hospitals, for example) and the payor side (insurance companies) are beginning to meld, with some hospitals purchasing insurance companies and some insurance companies purchasing hospitals and physician practices. Nevertheless, for the purpose of providing a primer to the industry, the categorization is valid.

Providers

The provider sector is just what it sounds like: those individuals or entities directly rendering health care services. On the individual side this includes doctors, nurses, therapists (respiratory, occupational, physical, audiological), psychologists, and any other individuals directly providing health care services. Providers may also be institutions, such as hospitals and nursing homes. Institutional providers may also be specialty facilities like rehabilitation hospitals, cancer care centers, cardiology hospitals, and ambulatory surgery centers. Recently, walk-in clinics, sometimes sponsored by health systems or drugstore chains, have entered the ranks of providers.

As you would expect, each type of provider has its own unique business and legal issues, requiring its health care attorney to have a concentrated body of knowledge in order to advise it. Individual providers, for example, may face licensure issues, disciplinary issues, contractual disputes, and liability concerns. Beyond these unique health law issues, however, they may also face real estate issues, tax concerns (personal or corporate), corporate law issues (shareholder issues, for instance), and the need for basic contract review services. The health lawyer brings his or her unique expertise to bear in these general matters, recognizing that health law regulations potentially impact whom a physician can rent office space from and how much rent can be paid, for example, or set limitations on how a provider may pursue collection efforts from a patient.

Institutional providers, too, offer significant legal issues to work through. State and federal governments, and sometimes local communities, heavily regulate these providers. Indeed, it is believed that health care providers are second only to the nuclear power industry in the degree of regulation that they face. Further, given their complexity, institutional providers typically face a range of sophisticated business issues, necessitating continual legal advice as they work to serve the community in their market.

Suppliers

The health care supplier side of the industry is in many ways the silent workhorse: behind the scenes but vital to the operations of health care providers. Suppliers are those entities that provide necessary items or services for health care to function, but often are not visible to health care consumers. The supplier industry is very broad, encompassing everything from laundry and food services to medical supplies and equipment to information technology and environmental services. Sometimes the subject of direct regulation, such as medical devices and equipment, suppliers are also significantly impacted by the laws directed toward providers and payors, as anything that impacts the quantity, quality, or payment of health care ultimately will affect the domain of suppliers in some way.

Payors

Although in the typical consumer transaction the "purchaser/user" and the "payor" are combined—I need a shirt so I buy one and pay for it—this is generally not the case in health care. For individuals with health insurance (still the vast majority of Americans even though we have a significant un-/ underinsured population), the purchasing/using function and the payment function are separate. Indeed, there is even a debate about who the purchaser is. Is it the employer who may have purchased insurance on the employee's behalf, is it the doctor who orders tests and treatment for the patient, or is it the patient him- or herself? Payors—private insurance companies, health maintenance organizations and other types of entities, or governmental programs such as Medicare or Medicaid—pay for the care provided. In doing so, they impose significant regulations (Medicare and Medicaid) or stringent contractual requirements that significantly impact whether and how health care will be provided, what will be provided, where it will be provided, and when it will be provided. Understanding the payment mechanisms used by governmental and private payors, and the regulatory/contractual restraints imposed as a condition for receiving payment, is an essential body of knowledge for any health care attorney.

Pharmaceuticals

While always an important component of the health care industry, the pharmaceutical and medical device sector has bloomed in the past 15 years. Today, about 10 percent of federal health care dollars are spent on pharmaceuticals,[3] and this figure is sure to grow. Further, with Medicare coverage extended to pharmaceuticals in 2006, the regulatory issues confronting pharma—always significant—have greatly expanded. Attorneys working in the pharmaceutical arena are faced with laws flowing from food and drug law, public health law, intellectual property law, Medicare and Medicaid, and many other areas beyond the bevy of traditional legal issues that arise with a large corporate client. Too, these companies often work internationally, requiring expertise in laws of other countries as well as in U.S. laws governing foreign business transactions.

Major Forces Impacting Health Care

Although familiarity with the industry structure is important as you consider your niche in health law, it is also imperative to understand the significant forces impacting the industry, because many of these forces may provide direction or a building block for a successful career in health law. While a full recitation of forces impacting every sector of the health care industry

---

3. Aetna, *The Facts About Rising Health Care Costs*, http://www.aetna.com/health-reform-connection/aetnas-vision/facts-about-costs.html (last visited Mar. 24, 2014) (stating that 10.01 percent of the health care spending budget is spent on prescription drugs). *See* Ctrs. for Medicare & Medicaid Servs., *The National Health Expenditures Price Index*, http://www.cms.gov/Research-Statistics-Data-and-Systems/Statistics-Trends-and-Reports/NationalHealthExpendData/downloads/tables.pdf (last visited Mar. 24, 2014).

is beyond the scope of this discussion, the following major categories are worthy of consideration.

Demographics

Life expectancy is increasing (a good thing!), and the percentage of the elderly population is rapidly growing. Indeed, one of the fastest-growing segments of the U.S. population is what is considered the "old elderly"— those over age 85. These demographics have a significant impact on the need for senior care service providers (both individual and institutional), chronic care service providers, durable medical equipment providers (walkers, wheelchairs, etc.), and medical device suppliers (artificial knees, hips, etc.), just to name a few. Pharmaceutical use is likely to continue accelerating as people live longer, with more chronic ailments, and look to medications to assist them in maintaining quality of life.

Technology

It is very obvious that technology is exploding in the health care arena. Electronic medical records are becoming the norm, medical apps are expanding, medical technology is moving from a central location to the bedside and ultimately to the home, and home monitoring is rapidly advancing.

Competition

Health care delivery and supply are becoming heavily competitive as payment mechanisms change and costs continue to decrease, but payment amounts decline. As this book is being written, federal health care reform (discussed later in this chapter) is being implemented, unleashing a massive consolidation wave among providers to drive down costs through economies of scale, integrate services to respond to quality standards, and "bulk up" to confront a rapidly changing future.

Quality

Study after study has demonstrated significant differences in how the same medical conditions are treated across the country. These disparities will no longer be allowed to continue. Further, historically, little attention has been placed on the quality of care outcome being achieved. This is undergoing rapid change, with poor quality being financially punished and high quality of care providers being rewarded.

Integration

The boundaries between provider, supplier, payor, and to a lesser extent, pharma are receding, with entities being formed that share many of these attributes. In part, this consolidation is resulting from movements to pay providers on the basis of their ability to maintain the health of a population, as opposed to paying them for services provided when someone becomes ill or injured. How these various components of the health care industry will come together, and the contours of these relationships, will require significant thinking and work by health care attorneys.

Budgetary Pressure

As previously discussed, health care is expensive and increasingly taking an ever larger piece of federal and state budgets. We are at a point where this can no longer continue. Federal and state efforts to drive down health care expenditures, coupled with the employer trend to impose more health care costs on employees, is going to have a profound effect on how health care is delivered.

PPACA

The Patient Protection and Affordable Care Act (commonly referred to as "PPACA" or the "ACA"), the federal health reform initiative, is directly and indirectly reshaping one of the largest sectors of the U.S. economy. With a statute in excess of 2,000 pages, the breadth and depth of regulatory changes impacting all sectors within health care is unprecedented. Further, the industry's response to the law—the indirect effects—is likewise significant. These changes will take years to filter through the system, let alone the continued retooling to further shape federal, state, and private (employer) reform efforts.

Your Career in Health Law

Given the unprecedented change impacting the industry, there simply is no better time to enter the field of health law. The industry will continue to expand and change, spawning the need for attorneys well versed in industry knowledge and adept at working with their clients to anticipate needs and respond to a rapidly evolving, challenging environment. The remaining chapters discuss specific practice areas within health law that you might pursue, various practice settings for health law, and specific strategies to begin or further your career. Regardless of which path you pursue, you will find personal and professional fulfillment in the health law field.

Chapter 2

Where to Find a Job as a Health Lawyer—By Content Area

As you read in Chapter 1, the field of health law is vast and unique because it is a set of laws and regulations that govern an entire industry, not just a specific type of case or transaction. The field can be broken down into many subsets. This chapter will describe and distinguish the many subset content areas in health law. Focusing on these content areas can help would-be health lawyers further identify and align their areas of interest and expertise.

Antitrust

As the health care field continues to grow at a rapid pace, so does competition. Competition in the health field is controversial, resulting in opportunities for health law attorneys to deal with antitrust issues, from both the prosecutorial and defense perspectives, or simply in terms of client counseling. Antitrust issues often arise in connection with joint ventures, mergers and acquisitions, medical staff privileging decisions, and health trade association activities. The three federal laws comprising the antitrust area are the Sherman Act, the Clayton Act, and the Federal Trade Commission Act. Together, these laws prohibit attempts at price fixing, monopolization, restraint of trade, and other harms to competition. Beyond the statutes, antitrust has an exceptionally rich body of case law. Successful antitrust attorneys are skilled at, and enjoy, being able to delve into the business (market) and marketing strategies of their clients and applying case law to facts.

Two federal agencies enforce antitrust laws: the Department of Justice Antitrust Division (DOJ) and the Federal Trade Commission (FTC). In recognition of the characteristics and rapidly changing nature of the health care market, the DOJ and FTC have issued joint policy statements to explain their enforcement of mergers and other joint activities in the health care field.[1] Examining this joint statement can give you an appreciation for the work associated with antitrust counseling and enforcement.

Privileging decisions for medical staff can also raise antitrust concerns. When health care institutions determine whether a medical staff member receives privileges at the institution (meaning the ability to admit and treat patients at the facility), these decisions are made upon recommendation of current medical staff of the institution. Because medical staff within an institution may end up competing for patients, these decisions are scrutinized for potential anticompetitive behavior.

Antitrust issues potentially arise whenever transactions occur that have an impact on the competitive landscape, although the government will only act on those activities having a material, negative impact on competition. For example, if two hospitals in an area with two or three hospitals wish to merge, antitrust issues are likely to come to the fore.[2]

More recently, significant antitrust work has been focused in the hospital and physician integration area. As hospitals begin pulling together physician groups who have been competitors, to develop what are termed "clinically integrated" services involving heightened standards of care, significant government attention has been focused on these arrangements to assure that they do not foster anticompetitive behavior.

---

1. U.S. DEP'T OF JUSTICE, FED. TRADE COMM'N, STATEMENTS OF ANTITRUST ENFORCEMENT POLICY IN HEALTH CARE (Aug. 1996), *available at* http://www.justice.gov/atr/public/guidelines/0000.htm.

2. *See, e.g.*, Press Release, State of Connecticut Attorney General George Jepsen, Attorney General Jepsen Completes Antitrust Investigation of Proposed Yale-New Haven, St. Raphael Merger (June 1, 2012), *available at* http://www.ct.gov/ag/cwp/view.asp?A=2341&Q=505376.

As the impact of health reform initiatives continues to drive all sectors of the health care industry toward greater consolidation, attention to antitrust counseling, and conversely antitrust enforcement, is certain to grow.

Trade associations, of which the health care industry has many, can also raise antitrust concerns because of the opportunity they provide for competitors to exchange information. A good example of this is where data is shared among members of a trade association. To some extent, enforcement involving associations has largely played itself out, as the guidelines under which associations may share information have become routinized. As competitors continually aggregate in the market to jointly bid on insurance contracts, however, counseling in this arena—centered on avoiding allegations of price fixing—is likely to be front and center.

Attorneys in private practice play a role in counseling clients as transactions and arrangements are structured so as to ensure compliance with federal and state antitrust laws. Firms also work to defend clients alleged to have run afoul of these laws. Large and midsize firms may have dedicated practice groups focused on antitrust. Additionally, attorneys working within health care organizations and trade associations often take an active role in preventing anticompetitive behavior in order to assist their client in avoiding scrutiny.

On the prosecutorial side, both the DOJ and FTC employ attorneys to enforce the antitrust laws. Additionally, each state has developed antitrust laws and standards, many of which align with federal laws. Therefore, each state may also have a prosecutorial role in policing anticompetitive activity within that state. This provides an opportunity for employment at the state level.

CAREER PROFILE

DAVID MARX JR.
Partner
McDermott Will & Emery LLP

My practice as a partner in the Antitrust Practice Group at McDermott is a mix of advising clients, both individuals and corporations, on

Continued

CAREER PROFILE *Continued*

the competitive and legal implications of their business operations and representing them in connection with litigation or government investigations, criminal and civil, arising out of or relating to their conduct. A primary reason that my practice is so interesting is that the clients I work with compete in a wide range of industries and businesses, one of which is the health care field. As a result, I represent all forms of health care providers, hospitals and health care systems, physicians, pharmaceutical manufacturers, and commercial insurance companies. I represent providers that are privately owned, for-profit and not-for-profit, as well as governmentally owned (such as legislatively created government hospital districts). And the questions that I deal with on a daily basis present not only "legal" but also regulatory and economic issues.

The federal and state antitrust laws are intended to preserve and promote price and non-price competition (such as customer service, product development, and innovation), and they apply to all health care providers. They are enforced by both federal and state government agencies (Federal Trade Commission, Antitrust Division of the U.S. Department of Justice, and state Attorneys General), as well as private parties who, when they are harmed by anticompetitive conduct, may file a complaint seeking monetary damages or equitable relief against those who engaged in the allegedly unlawful activities. The penalties for antitrust violations, criminal or civil, are severe—jail time and fines for individuals, criminal fines up to and sometimes exceeding $100 million for corporations, and monetary damages and civil penalties that frequently amount to hundreds of millions of dollars. The legal fees for defending a party under investigation or charged with an antitrust violation invariably run into seven or eight figures (to the left of the decimal point)—which makes it even more important that I provide knowledgeable, comprehensive, understandable, and practical advice that enables clients to achieve their legitimate business objectives without creating unwanted exposure to the antitrust laws.

Presently, I spend about 50 percent of my time managing and participating in litigation matters for my health care clients; the rest of my time is devoted to counseling clients on their business operations. The litigation side of the practice is split, though not necessarily evenly, between enforcement activities (investigations in advance of litigation) and civil litigation, where I represent defendants in class actions or cases filed by an individual plaintiff, private or governmental. Most of the litigation occurs in federal court or before the Federal Trade Commission, which is an administrative agency, and because we represent health care clients across the United States, my practice requires extensive travel, which is not as glamorous as it might appear to be.

Counseling usually entails answering the question, "Can I do that?" where "that" might be acquiring or merging or entering into a joint venture with a local competitor, entering into an exclusive contract with a physician group to provide services at a hospital, forming or operating a provider network (or Accountable Care Organization) to single-signature contract with commercial insurance companies, or lobbying a government agency to adopt a rule or regulation (or otherwise do something) that could adversely affect a competitor. Before responding to what appears to be an innocently simple question, however, I have to develop a complete understanding of my client's business, the markets in which it competes, the nature of competition in those markets (that is, who my client's competitors are, how they compete, who the consumers or customers in that market are, and what economic factors influence competition in those markets), the reasons (both good, or procompetitive, and bad, or anticompetitive) my client wants to engage in the conduct it is inquiring about, and the likely competitive effects (again, procompetitive and anticompetitive) that may result from that conduct. Without the answers to those broad, and frequently complex, questions, I cannot be sure that my advice will be both right and useful. When it comes to antitrust counseling, the advice that I have to give often is something like, "You should not do exactly what you are asking, but there is something else you can do that will enable you to achieve your legitimate business objective and reduce your antitrust exposure." In other words, a big part of my job is finding a way "to get to yes." Clients hate it when I say no without offering an alternative, favorable response to their question.

Because health care is delivered on a local basis, each case and counseling question is different—even if the overarching legal, regulatory, or economic issues are the same. For example, the answer to the question whether the merger of two health care systems or hospitals in Chicago will violate the antitrust laws raises different factual and economic issues than the same question with respect to two competing hospitals in Rockford, Illinois, or Toledo, Ohio. In health care, every market is different and, therefore, requires individual factual analysis. That makes the work interesting and varied.

The litigation practice, on the other hand, has changed over time, as people have shifted from communicating on paper to corresponding "electronically." The vast quantity of "electronically stored information," coupled with the broad scope of discovery generally allowed in antitrust cases, means that I (or those working with me on a case or investigation) now spend an extensive amount of time engaging in "discovery about discovery" that generally has nothing to do with a case's factual or legal merits. That is, perhaps, the least interesting part of the litigation process, though it is an expensive component of it.

Continued

Because antitrust law represents the intersection of law and economics, I spend a lot of time working with experts in other fields—economists, financial analysts, business consultants, and advisors with expertise in health care–related issues. I have often joked that, in my next life, I want to return as a consulting or testifying economist, because their hourly rates are higher than lawyers' and they are far less accountable to clients for the results of their work! Similarly, I have frequent interaction with the governmental antitrust enforcement agencies, which sometimes don't fully appreciate how expensive (both directly and indirectly) and time-consuming their investigations can be for clients to defend (or respond to as a third party).

One of the most challenging aspects of my antitrust practice is the fact that health care is delivered in a market where prices are sometimes competitively set and sometimes regulated, and the government is both the regulator and the largest consumer of health care providers' services. That complicates the economic analysis of the competitive implications of a health care provider's conduct, which makes it harder to render an opinion about the legality of proposed conduct with a high degree of certainty. That does, however, make the work both more challenging and intellectually stimulating.

Corporate, Transactional, and Contract Law

The entities involved in the delivery of health care are all businesses and, thus, face a number of issues in corporate, transactional, and contract law. Indeed, the scope, scale, and complexity of many health care clients mean that attorneys who specialize in the corporate/transactional arena routinely become involved in extremely sophisticated work. Further, because of the highly regulated nature of the health care industry, rare is the case where a situation involves "merely" the application of general corporate law or contracting principles. Accordingly, attorneys working in this area must have a solid grasp of health care business fundamentals, coupled with expertise in corporate law and governance transactions, and contract law. Skills in contract drafting are also essential. This area of law typically involves significant client counseling. Corporate/transactional health care attorneys often find this arena one of the most rewarding in health law, as there is a real opportunity to work closely with executives to formulate key business strategies.

Transactions and contracts for health care organizations are governed by a vast number of federal and state laws. Corporate law issues arise in every major transaction undertaken by health care organizations. Examples run the gamut from the establishment of health care organizations and systems, acquisitions, and joint ventures to financings, facility construction, and business expansion.

A keen understanding of the health care business environment and general corporate/transactional law is not enough, however. Corporate health care attorneys also must recognize and counsel on the interplay of health care law and regulations and a myriad of other laws, regulations, and standards that must be accounted for when counseling in the corporate/transactional arena. Related issues include state and federal health planning requirements, licensure obligations, and a variety of other business concerns.

The entire health delivery system, particularly where third-party reimbursement is concerned, is premised on a series of contracts, generally with government agencies, insurers, physicians, and institutional providers of care and suppliers of services. Types of contracts often used in health care delivery include payment and reimbursement, labor and employment, supplies and services, affiliation, and those drafted for the specific transactions detailed above. Contract law is thus directly involved in most health care practices. Again, the highly regulated nature of health care means that every contract must be drafted and reviewed with an eye toward ensuring compliance with health care–specific laws and practices.

Every health care transaction or contract requires representation for each party involved. Health care attorneys represent government agencies, insurers, physicians and other health care professionals, institutional providers of care, and suppliers. This type of practice is generally conducted by in-house legal counsel and attorneys at law firms overseen by in-house counsel. It should be noted that, given the complexity of the health care industry, some attorneys specialize in representation of a particular type of party (such as ambulatory outpatient facilities and hospitals) while others may specialize in particular types of transactions (such as joint ventures).

As might be surmised, large transactions raise a host of complex issues requiring in-depth analysis beyond that of corporate health law counsel. Often, attorneys with specialty expertise in antitrust, fraud and abuse, labor, insurance, tax, and most notably, regulatory law (among others) will become involved.

Criminal Law

Several areas within health law also involve counseling to avoid, as well as prosecuting and defending, criminal activities. The largest application of criminal law in the field falls under fraud in the delivery of health care. This area involves violations of the federal health care Anti-Kickback Statute[3] (which criminalizes payments made in return for a referral or for ordering a service or supply paid for by Medicare, Medicaid, or any other federal governmental health care program), the False Claims Act,[4] and other federal laws including mail and wire fraud, money laundering, and conspiracy. Separate and apart from prohibited activities that have been criminalized is a significant range of activities that are prosecuted by the government through civil proceedings as well as through exclusion from participation in federal insurance programs. Because criminal and civil actions can be brought at the same time and an activity may lend itself to enforcement criminally, civilly, and/or through exclusion, health lawyers working in this area must be experts in general criminal law (typically "white collar" offenses) along with health care–specific laws.

In addition, state health care laws in this arena typically parrot federal laws, requiring attorneys to be well versed on the state's approach to prosecution in any particular area.

---

3. Social Security Act, 42 U.S.C.A. § 1320a-7b (West 2011).
4. False Claims Act, 31 U.S.C.A. § 3729 (West 2012).

A core part of health law practice is advising clients on how to conduct their business in ways that do not run afoul of criminal law, particularly the Anti-Kickback Statute. For example, in any transaction between health care entities involving an exchange of value—from creating a contract between a hospital and a doctor to purchasing medical supplies or ordering pharmaceuticals to be used by Medicare patients—the Anti-Kickback Statute can be triggered. Attorneys both in-house and in private practice work to set up entities and contracts so as to avoid these issues and to establish compliance programs that prevent fraud and abuse within institutions. Attorneys also represent health care clients, individual and institutional, when they are under investigation by the government and facing trial.

On the government side, attorneys within the Department of Justice and the Department of Health and Human Services (HHS) Office of Inspector General investigate and prosecute criminal activity in the delivery of health care. State and local governments may also investigate and bring claims for fraud and abuse. Medicaid and Medicare fraud are prime targets for fraud investigation and prosecution.

Disability and Elder Law

Disability law intersects with health care law. Persons with disabilities often need to access health care services frequently. Government health programs, such as Medicaid, provide funding for health care for more than 8 million non-elderly adults.[5] Many individuals qualifying for Medicaid also qualify for Social Security Income assistance.[6] Attorneys often represent disabled individuals in the procurement of these benefits, which include application processes and verification by health care professionals. These legal services are provided by attorneys in private practice and often by attorneys working

---

5. CTRS. FOR MEDICARE & MEDICAID SERVS., *Individuals with Disabilities*, http://www
.medicaid.gov/Medicaid-CHIP-Program-Information/By-Population/People-with-Disabilities
/Individuals-with-Disabilities.html (last visited Mar. 24, 2014).

6. *Id.*

for public interest organizations. A strong knowledge of administrative law processes is essential for attorneys working in this area.

Disability law can also bring attorneys into the mental health/behavioral health arena. Laws and practices pertaining to access to medication and treatment dominate this field of practice. In addition, antidiscrimination laws, family law (including custody and guardianship), and school law, among others, can weave through this health law specialty, making it a very rewarding area for individuals who thrive on advising largely individual, as opposed to institutional, clients.

The need for attorneys who understand elder law issues continues to grow. Persons older than age 65 in the United States currently make up 12.9 percent of the population and that number is predicted to increase to 19 percent by 2030, with an expected population of 72 million people 65 and over.[7] Although elder law is defined generally by the issues arising for the population it serves, many areas of elder law practice arise in the health law context. Most often, these involve planning for how elderly persons will navigate the health care system, including advance directives, guardianship, and arrangements for long-term care. Elder law attorneys also help procure funding for health care through private insurance, Medicaid and/or Medicare, and Social Security disability funding. Sadly, elder abuse (physical, emotional, and/or financial) is another common area for legal representation. Attorneys working in this area often work in private practice and handle these health care issues as well as general estate planning. Elder law, like disability law, is another area in which many attorneys work in the public interest law setting.

---

7. U.S. DEP'T OF HEALTH & HUMAN SERVS., ADMIN. ON AGING, *Aging Statistics*, http://www .aoa.gov/Aging_Statistics/ (last visited Mar. 24, 2014).

CAREER PROFILE

Joe Monahan
Cofounder
Monahan Law Group LLC

Persons 65 years of age or older numbered 39.6 million in 2009, or 12.9 percent of the U.S. population, and by 2030 the elderly population is expected to grow to over 72 million persons, or about 19 percent of the population. This aging of the population is fueling a strong interest in elder law. Seminars, workshops, and career advisors highlight the opportunities in the field and encourage lawyers to be trained as an elder law attorney.

So what is an elder law lawyer? It is a term that encompasses many different areas of the law that focuses on issues which impact persons who are elderly and, for some practitioners, persons with disabilities. Elder law is most commonly associated with three broad areas: estate planning, Medicaid and disability planning, and guardianship and commitment. Within the three broader areas are nursing home issues, elder abuse, retirement planning, long-term care, insurance issues, real estate, mortgage issues, and age discrimination in employment and housing. Elder law is broad and provides multiple opportunities for practice.

Our law firm includes eight lawyers, two paralegals, and usually one or two law students. We represent 70 hospitals throughout the state of Illinois, mostly in the Chicago metropolitan area. We are retained to address patient care litigation issues that arise in the hospitals. These include guardianship, mental health, commitment, elder abuse, posthospital placement issues, and the like.

We are brought in on a number of patient issues, which often will be broader than issues that impact persons who are elderly. These issues can range from pre-birth to post-death. Our hospital practice often goes beyond what is typically considered elder law.

Because I am the managing partner of our law firm, I have a myriad of administrative tasks that demand my attention. These include marketing the practice; recruiting and maintaining staff; supervising human resources, payroll, and accounting; and overseeing the general operation of the firm.

I usually do two or three major trials every year. In the last two years, I orally argued one case in the Illinois Supreme Court and two in the Illinois Appellate Court. I regularly appear in courts throughout the metropolitan area on emergency motions related to patient issues regarding guardianship, mental health, elder abuse, or child abuse issues.

Our firm is committed to pro bono service. We encourage all of our lawyers to do pro bono work. Our lawyers participate on a number of bar association committees, serve as directors for not-for-profit boards,

Continued

and regularly accept appointments to do pro bono litigation from the courts and Chicago Volunteer Legal Services.

My long-term pro bono legal commitment has been to the National Association of Social Workers (NASW). Currently, I serve as the President of the Board of the NASW Malpractice Insurance Company. In the past, I served on the National Board of Directors and as Trustee of the Legal Assistance Fund for NASW. I also regularly lecture for bar association groups, do trainings for local community agencies, and serve as a director for a local not-for-profit community foundation.

Without doubt, I have the best job in the world. My job is challenging, dynamic, and rewarding. I work with very smart, dedicated professionals who have all made their jobs their life's work. We do excellent work and push each other to do the best we can for our clients. I am proud of our work and am happy to be concentrating in the practice of elder law and its related fields.

Health Policy and Advocacy, Bioethics, and Public Health

Health Policy and Advocacy

Health policy work involves not only the study of current or prospective laws and regulations but also proposals for new laws or changes to existing ones. In the highly regulated field of health care, there are many individuals and organizations concerned with health policy that seek to have a voice in what laws are developed and how they are implemented. Given the rapidly changing world of health care, there is a constant need for analysis of how new laws and policies will affect the stakeholders in the health care system, including all types of providers, institutions, and consumers.

The "practice" of health policy is broad. Most commonly, policy work in the health care context involves analyzing laws and regulations, both existing and prospective, to determine their practical impact on the health care industry. Attorneys working in this area may also become involved in drafting white papers, policy briefs, and legislation. They often provide internal and external presentations, typically balancing issue education with advocacy.

Policy work is usually done from the viewpoint of each stakeholder, but it can also be done in academic or other neutral settings. For example, attorneys and other professionals at trade associations work to develop policy supportive of their members. These policy analyses and positions are then used to disseminate information about the laws to providers, institutions, and consumers and to influence lawmakers, regulators, and the judiciary.

Attorneys working in health policy serve in a number of contexts and practice settings. Many attorneys working in public interest organizations analyze and advocate for policy changes to improve legal outcomes for their clients. These organizations can vary in size from local disability rights organizations to national associations such as AARP (formerly the American Association of Retired Persons). Many associations connected to the health care industry undertake policy work. These range from associations representing specific types of health care providers, both individually (American Medical Association) and institutionally (American Hospital Association and the Pharmaceutical Research and Manufacturers of America), to payors (America's Health Insurance Plans).

Many organizations also seek opportunities to become involved in influencing health policy through legislative influence (lobbying) or judicial action (amicus briefs or impact litigation). Attorneys also contribute to policy through the drafting and editing of legislation and regulations. This can be done for government institutions, individual political and government leaders, or nongovernmental organizations that aid in drafting legislation and regulations.

Bioethics

The field of bioethics includes the study of the ethical, legal, and social implications of biological research, most often in the medical context. Bioethical issues often involve the intersection of science, law, policy, religion, cultural norms and values, and economics. Although bioethics is a discipline distinct from law and a law license is not a requirement for being a bioethicist, there are many intersections between the two fields. Many hotly contested topics in health care fall within the sphere of bioethics, including stem cell research, genomics, reproductive rights, and end-of-life issues. Because advances in science and medical technology occur across the world, work in bioethics can be international as different countries develop and then address the implications of advances.

Attorneys desiring to work exclusively (or even primarily) in the field of bioethics can expect to conduct significant research on and analysis of the legal implications of emerging science and medical technology, developments in health care laws and regulations, and allocation and appropriateness of resources in medical decision making. Many attorneys interested in a strong bioethics focus pursue careers in academia. These include teaching, researching, and writing on bioethics issues in undergraduate programs and postgraduate programs in law, ethics, philosophy, and health sciences. In addition, attorneys may find employment with bioethics consulting groups and ethics committees, as well as institutional review boards charged with overseeing human subject research. Large trade associations, such as the American Medical Association and the Catholic Health Association, have significant depth in their ethics counsel offices.

Although it is not an area of exclusive focus, hospital/health system counsel (typically in-house, but occasionally outside counsel) are routinely called upon to address bioethical issues. Common situations include end-of-life decision making (especially involving family disputes over patient wishes), treatment for emancipated minors, and to a lesser extent, fetal-maternal conflicts.

Public Health

Public health law often overlaps with health policy and bioethics. Like bioethics, public health law is a field that operates at the intersection of medicine, science, policy, and law. Attorneys working in the field of public health research and analyze public health issues and the impact of existing and potential laws and regulations on public health. Public health initiatives can range in scope from local communities to national and international issues.

Many attorneys working in the public health arena are employed by the government. State, and sometimes local, governments have public health agencies that employ attorneys to work alongside medical experts to produce policies and regulations that maximize public health and ensure appropriate responses to public health crises. These attorneys also routinely advise on the myriad of activities housed within state public health agencies, including licensure, public safety, wellness, and health planning initiatives. Public health counsel routinely become involved in drafting legislation, advising the executive and legislative branches of state government, convening public educational forums, and serving as a resource to other state and local agencies.

Some nongovernmental agencies engage in similar work promoting public health and wellness and preventing disease. Attorneys working for these organizations provide legal advice on proper initiatives and analyze and develop policies to increase public health.

Several federal agencies, such as the Centers for Disease Control and Prevention and the Occupational Safety and Health Administration, focus on public health issues and employ attorneys to work in this area. For more information on careers in government, see Chapter 3, which describes careers by practice setting.

Insurance

The delivery of health care is closely linked with insurance, both private and public. Many attorneys and firms count private insurers among their clients, and many attorneys also advise their health care clients on their relationships with insurers. Both state and federal laws regulate private and public insurance. Therefore, this is a broad area of practice.

A fundamental dynamic of health reform is the merging of two previously separate functions and disciplines—provider and insurer. As Medicare and private payors have moved toward risk-based contracting, many health care systems have moved to begin, or acquire, insurance companies. In a few instances, the reverse has occurred—one insurer, for example, purchased a health system while another acquired a large medical practice.

In short, the future appears very bright for health care attorneys interested in insurance law as the scope of this area is expanding rapidly. Often this work is highly technical. Significant time must be accorded to understanding state insurance codes and the administrative processes embedded in them.

Attorneys may advise on everything from insurance company startups to "captive" insurance companies (for example, for malpractice coverage) to insurance compliance, among other things.

Attorneys in this area also advise on ERISA (Employment Retirement Income Security Act) law and its interface with state insurance codes. Legal counsel in these areas often extends to employee benefits as well.

Knowledgeable health law attorneys with insurance expertise are needed in a number of settings and will be in increasing demand. Obviously insurance companies and government need this expertise. Increasingly, however, large health care systems and other organizations positioning themselves to assume a population's health risk will need insurance counsel. It is likely that strong growth will continue in the benefits design area, meaning that practices with this expertise should be seeking to add people with an insurance law skill set.

CAREER PROFILE

Colleen Burns
Special Counsel for Health Policy
Office of the Governor

My interest in health care began after I graduated from college and went to work for U.S. Senator Hillary Rodham Clinton. I worked in her New York City office as a liaison between her constituents and federal agencies. I responded to inquiries and resolved difficulties for New York residents in need. I was then responsible for advising the senator on the issues that affected these residents in the areas of health care, housing, and Social Security. I found my work for the senator's office very fulfilling but also frustrating. When an individual contacted the senator's office for help with an issue, I was constricted to helping only those residents whose problems involved a federal agency. Many of the residents I worked with had issues that went beyond the reach of a federal agency: homelessness (at the time, the wait in New York City for public housing was 13 years), unemployment, mental illness and substance abuse, and chronic illness, to name just a few. I was frustrated by my inability to address these non-federal issues for the residents with which I dealt. I wanted to do more. This desire ultimately led me to the decision to go to law school and pursue a career in health law.

I am a native Chicagoan and was excited about the prospect of returning to my hometown to attend law school. I chose Loyola University School of Law because of its well-known health law program. Having a focus for my studies in law school allowed me to explore other areas of the law through externships. I deliberately sought out diverse experiences. I externed for two federal judges, worked for an education nonprofit, worked for a Chicago hospital, volunteered in Cook County juvenile detention, and taught a class on the law to a group of high school senior boys. These experiences allowed me to gain exposure to many areas of the law and reaffirmed my commitment to health law.

I knew I wanted to work on health policy but was not entirely sure what kind of health policy jobs existed, especially outside Washington, D.C. After graduating from law school I spent a short time working for a small union labor and employment law firm. I greatly enjoyed my time there working on matters that affected everyday working men and women.

Just after I graduated, however, I had responded to a job posting that came through Loyola: The Department of Insurance was looking for someone to help implement the Affordable Care Act (ACA). I promptly forgot about it until about 6 months later when I received a call asking me to come in and discuss the position. Ultimately, I was asked to join a small team of people responsible for implementing the ACA for the state. The Department of Insurance, as the state agency responsible for enforcing our insurance laws and regulating the insurance industry, was the perfect place to house the state's efforts to implement the Affordable Care Act.

As the team's only attorney, I was responsible for ensuring compliance with applicable state and federal laws and advising the department on legislative and policy agenda items related to the ACA. In the beginning, I was responsible for helping the department implement all aspects of the ACA, including establishing a premium rate review program and reviewing the department's medical loss ratio standards. However, as it became clear that the affordable health insurance exchanges were taking up more and more of our time, I was asked to lead the department's efforts to establish a Health Insurance Exchange in Illinois. This meant that I was responsible for serving as a liaison to the federal government and all state agencies participating in the Marketplace project, including the Governor's Office, the Department of Healthcare and Family Services, the Department of Human Services, the Department of Public Health, and the Office of Health Information Technology. I was also responsible for managing all of the department's federal grants under the ACA, which provided money to states to implement these important programs.

A large part of our efforts turned toward helping the Illinois General Assembly to understand why we needed legislation to become a state-based exchange. Under the ACA, all states must set up an exchange. If they fail

Continued

CAREER PROFILE *Continued*

to do so, the federal government will run the exchange. To establish a state-based exchange, a state is required to have legislation that provides for a governance structure (a new state agency, a quasi-government agency, or a nonprofit) and a means for financing the exchange (in most states this was accomplished through an assessment on insurance carriers).

All interested stakeholders in Illinois, including the health insurance industry, were clear that they wanted Illinois to have control of the exchange. Unfortunately, we could not get legislation passed in time for Illinois to run its own exchange in the first year of operations (2014). Instead, Illinois chose to pursue a partnership arrangement in which the state would take on the responsibility for some portions of the exchange (certifying the health plans that would be sold in the state and providing consumer education) and the federal government would run the rest. This option was given to states that were moving toward a state-based exchange but needed more time for implementation.

Our team spent all of 2013 preparing for open enrollment in October, even though the federal government would be running the website. We focused our attention on ensuring that all of the health plans submitted for approval were given a thorough review and on ensuring that consumers in Illinois were educated about the Affordable Care Act and what it would mean for them.

Thereafter, I made the difficult decision to leave the Marketplace team and to take a position working for the Office of the Governor. In my new role, I work with the Governor's Senior Health Policy Advisor on all matters of health policy for the state. Our current focus has been on identifying innovative ways to change the delivery of health care in our state. We accomplished this by bringing together health care providers, health plans, large payors like the Cook County Health and Hospital System, and other interested stakeholders to discuss needed reforms to the health care system. This process ultimately led to the designing and drafting of the State Health Care Innovation Plan, which outlines the way Illinois seeks to accomplish these major changes. We intend to apply for a federal grant to help pay for the costs of taking on this challenge but are also looking for ways that we can change the system today, without any extra funding. It has been a tremendous learning experience and has allowed me to gain exposure to all aspects of our health system, including public health. I am looking forward to seeing Illinois become a leader in health care transformation.

Employment and Labor Law

The delivery of health care services is an extremely labor intensive enterprise, with the average hospital spending 50 percent of its revenue on staffing. Further, for the period 2004–2014, health care is expected to comprise 19 percent of all new jobs added to the U.S. economy. Many of the occupations with projections for fastest growth fall within the health care industry.[8] With a large and ever-growing workforce, the health care industry by definition raises a significant number of labor and employment issues.

As in all industries, health care employers must ensure employment conditions that comply with major labor and equal employment laws, including, but not limited to, the Civil Rights Act of 1964, the Fair Labor Standards Act, the Americans with Disabilities Act, and the Family and Medical Leave Act.[9] Additionally, the health care industry is confronted with unique labor laws and regulations, including special rules for unionization and collective bargaining.[10] Health care also presents particular issues with respect to maintaining a healthy and safe work environment for employees, with special attention to preventing illegal drug use and associated drug testing, the prevention of infection and the spread of disease, and safety and security.

Attorneys specializing in labor and employment issues in the health care setting work in a variety of contexts. In a general counsel's office and/or human resources department, significant time is spent on employment and labor law matters. Worthy of special attention are employment relationships between physicians and health care providers, as these often raise unique issues requiring special legal expertise (particularly in the areas of fraud and abuse and self-referral laws). Attorneys also represent individual physicians and other practitioners in their employment negotiations and terms.

Employment and labor law representation is often done by attorneys in-house as well as at firms ranging from small to large. Attorneys at small

---

8. U.S. Dep't of Labor, Emp't & Training Admin., High Growth Industry Profile—Health Care, http://www.doleta.gov/brg/indprof/healthcare_profile.cfm (last updated Mar. 8, 2010).

9. K. Bruce Stickler & Stephanie Dodge Gournis, Health L. Prac. Guide § 6:1 (2013), *available at* Westlaw.

10. *Id.*

firms are more likely to represent individual physicians and providers and small practice groups. Attorneys at mid-level and larger firms often represent larger physician and practitioner groups and institutions. Additionally, in-house attorneys within health care institutions and physician groups often deal with employment law issues from an institutional perspective.

Finally, given some of the unique labor laws impacting health care providers, unionization issues drive the need for specialty legal counsel from both an institutional as well as a collective bargaining point of view.

Life Sciences, Intellectual Property, and Food and Drug Law

Life sciences is emerging as a vastly important area of health law practice. Broadly defined, life sciences encompasses the intersection of health care regulation and the laws pertaining to the Food and Drug Administration (FDA), intellectual property, and privacy and security, all within a wrapper of medical technology. Life sciences encompasses the representation of biotechnology, pharmaceutical, medical device, and genomics companies, as well as any entity engaged in clinical or pharmaceutical/genomic research. Much of the growth in this area of legal practice stems from continuous development in pharmaceuticals and medical devices, new developments in genomics and personalized medicine, and the interaction of these issues with intellectual property law. All health care attorneys will find the life sciences arena a fascinating practice area, but especially those with a scientific background. And, while not required, attorneys who have passed the patent bar and wish to practice in this area will find their skills in demand.

Drugs and devices are highly regulated by the federal and, to some extent, state governments. Traditionally, the U.S. Food and Drug Administration has provided federal oversight for making and selling all pharmaceuticals and medical devices. This function includes monitoring research, tracking clinical trials, and overseeing the approval process for each drug and device used in the United States. In this role, the FDA employs many attorneys to handle this process.

Additionally, states are taking an increased role in overseeing the distribution of pharmaceuticals and medical devices within their borders. States have differing legislation governing these products and can have different agencies regulating them. State governments, therefore, also employ attorneys to oversee the distribution and sale of drugs and devices within their states. These can range from pharmacy boards to FDA-like agencies.

Likewise, each company or firm that researches, manufactures, and/or distributes drugs or devices must employ legal counsel to advise the firm on these processes. Large pharmaceutical and device companies often employ in-house attorneys and retain outside counsel. Smaller companies may only use outside counsel. Many attorneys at firms specialize in advising pharmaceutical and device companies through the FDA approval process and represent those companies if their products are found to be harmful.

As with other areas of health law, many attorneys represent companies in law firm settings. Each company involved with research, development, testing, marketing, or distribution of drugs and devices seeks the advice of counsel on these heavily regulated processes. Attorneys working at firms of all sizes advise on the regulatory process and on business transactions establishing and modifying these entities and represent them in litigation. There are, therefore, opportunities for attorneys to represent life sciences clients in many legal practice areas.

Compliance is another rapidly growing field within life sciences. Medical and pharmaceutical research and medical device development require oversight to ensure compliance with the many regulations in this area. Many pharmaceutical companies operate under Corporate Integrity Agreements executed as part of a settlement with the federal government requiring constant attention to compliance procedures. Additionally, academic and research institutions as well as hospitals often conduct medical research, thereby requiring research compliance officers. As new treatments and devices emerge, more expertise will be needed in these areas to help companies continue to comply with the complicated myriad of rules governing the life sciences sector.

Litigation

Many attorneys in health law practice are involved in litigation. As in any industry, disputes arise in health care between private parties and/or government entities. These can range from individual medical malpractice actions between patients and physicians to large government investigations and actions against multi-entity health care systems. Litigation practice can also range from a government investigation or filing of a claim to settlement or a full trial.

Most attorneys involved in health care litigation practice in law firm settings or work for the government. While some in-house attorneys help to manage litigation, it is rare for them to handle a litigation matter entirely on their own. Some litigators specialize in administrative litigation before components of the Department of Health and Human Services, the National Labor Relations Board, the Antitrust Division of the Department of Justice, and related government agencies. Other attorneys concentrate on litigation before state and federal judicial bodies. A litigation practice can encompass many areas or be limited to specialized issues, such as medical malpractice or insurance disputes.

Litigation also encompasses government and internal investigations. The government agencies tasked with enforcing health care and insurance laws and regulations regularly conduct investigations of health care entities. Fraud and abuse concerns comprise a large number of government investigations, including allegations of fraud in Medicare and Medicaid billing and improper financial relationships between physicians and entities under the so-called Stark law (prohibiting referrals to an entity in which the physician has a financial relationship).[11] Attorneys are involved on each side of these types of investigations, working for the government, at the entity under investigation, and for outside counsel employed by the entity.

Health care entities increasingly lead their own investigations when they suspect violations of health care laws and regulations. Attorneys within

---

11. Social Security Act, 42 U.S.C.A. § 1395nn (West 2010).

entities and working for outside law firms seek to uncover potential violations and defend any wrongdoing to the government.

One special note about medical malpractice litigation must be included here. Perhaps because it predates health law as a discipline, malpractice is often not considered part of the practice of health law, although arguably traditional health law "concepts"—informed consent, peer review, regulatory compliance, for example—can enter the malpractice arena. The dividing line between plaintiff and defense counsel in malpractice actions is especially stark in the health law context, given the historic concerns (fair or not) that the industry has had regarding excessive litigation.

Regulatory Law

Health care "regulatory law" is a vast area, as health care is one of the country's most heavily regulated industries. Federal, state, and even local governments create laws and regulations aimed to control who provides health care and how, when, and where that care is provided and paid for. Regulations cover virtually every aspect of the health care delivery system. To fully understand how regulation affects the entire industry, it is helpful to view the impact of regulations on all parties in health care.

For providers of health services, regulations dictate their organization and structure, certification, funding, accessibility of services, and the types of facilities in which services can be provided. Regulations also dictate the delivery of care, from restrictions on the types of facilities and personnel that can provide care to the situations in which it must be provided. All individual providers as well as institutions must be licensed to provide care. Regulations also require providers to balance the rights of patients with the duty to provide care.

Consumers also face regulations in choosing and receiving health care. Regulations help determine the quality of care consumers are entitled to receive and protect their privacy and health information. Regulations also determine a consumer's eligibility for third-party reimbursement for health services, including private and public insurance. Regulations also determine the type of consent that consumers must give to receive health care.

Third-party and government payors are also governed by an ever-increasing number of regulations on the state and federal level. The federal government's health care coverage programs, Medicare and Medicaid, are governed by a plethora of regulations. Each state plays an individual role in implementing Medicaid, and most states also have other types of public insurance for indigent citizens. Each state also places conditions and restrictions on private insurance companies offering insurance coverage to citizens within the state. The Patient Protection and Affordable Care Act[12] continues to add regulations focused on insurance at both the state and federal levels.

Attorneys work in the regulatory setting in a number of capacities. Federal and state governments employ individuals to oversee implementation of regulations and ensure their enforcement, taking legal action when they are not met. Providers, both individual and institutional, use attorneys, in-house and with outside firms, to ensure their operations comply with all regulations. Professional associations within the health care industry employ attorneys to help craft regulatory guidance for members.

Compliance plays an especially vital role in health care delivery because of the number of regulations that health care entities face. At the most basic level, the function of compliance departments and processes is to ensure that the entity follows all laws and regulations that apply to its existence and operations. Most health care providers employ compliance officers to devise and implement the organization's compliance program. Attorneys typically play a significant role in these programs.

Tax Law

Tax planning and analysis issues arise in nearly every type of health care industry transaction. Tax exemption is particularly relevant in health care because many organizations seek to achieve and maintain tax-exempt status.

---

12. Patient Protection and Affordable Care Act, 42 U.S.C.A. § 18001 (West 2010).

At the individual provider level, such as in a small group practice, issues of personal tax liability often drive the tax structure used by the entity, as the physicians' goals are generally to maximize individual income. Still, complexities associated with the Anti-Kickback Statute and, more importantly, the Stark federal anti–self-referral law, mean that appropriate compensation structures and relationships must be used to avoid liability exposure.

Tax issues also arise for physician practices or other similar individual provider entities during times of substantial organizational change, such as stock or major asset sales, changes of control, and dissolution.

About 80 percent of U.S. hospitals are nonprofit organizations recognized by the federal and relevant state governments as tax exempt. There are significant, sometimes intricate, laws that govern obtaining and maintaining tax-exempt status. Further, states are increasingly seeking to challenge property tax exemptions awarded to hospitals.

An important benefit of tax-exempt status is eligibility for tax-exempt financing, a significant funding source for most exempt organizations. As one might suppose, accessing this funding subjects the organization to still more laws and regulations governing the access to and use of finance proceeds.

Importantly, health care regulations, particularly those pertaining to fraud and abuse, dovetail with tax-exemption laws, such that failure to comply with fraud and abuse laws can jeopardize an organization's exempt status. Accordingly, a specialty health law/tax law niche has developed to enable further specialization for counsel wishing to practice at the intersection of these two areas.

Basic principles of tax-exemption law are a fundamental aspect of health law, and so at this level tax law is practiced by most in-house and outside health law attorneys. Specialty counsel is routinely sought for matters of particular difficulty, including financings, obtaining exempt status, and challenges to an organization's status, among other things.

Finally, for-profit providers, suppliers, and insurers will regularly consult health lawyers skilled in tax law to ensure that their tax strategies also comport with health care laws and regulations.

Chapter 3

Where to Find a Job as a Health Lawyer—By Practice Setting

This chapter describes and distinguishes among the many practice settings available to health lawyers, including law firms, government agencies (federal, state, and local), in-house providers, public interest organizations, trade associations, and business settings. This chapter also addresses venues where lawyers practice health law in litigation, regulatory, policy, and transactional work. Additionally, many individuals with a JD degree work in the health field without practicing law in the traditional sense. These alternative work settings are discussed in Chapter 4.

Law Firms

A high percentage of health law attorneys work for law firms, at least at the beginning of their careers. In fact, most health care organizations, hospitals, and other providers do not hire as in-house counsel lawyers who lack prior law firm or relevant governmental or consulting experience, because these organizations typically lack the resources to train new attorneys. Thus, most health law students focus their job search on law firms that either specialize in health law or have a health law practice.

For many years, attorneys practiced health law in law firms within the framework of other practice groups. For example, corporate law attorneys would represent health care providers or payors in mergers and acquisitions and other general transactional matters, without calling their work "health law." Over time, health law developed as its own distinct practice group within many law firms. There are still firms, however, that represent health care clients without identifying health law as a specific area of practice.

Law firms are businesses consisting of attorneys at different stages of their careers, from new associate attorneys to equity partners, as well as paralegals and administrative personnel who support the attorneys. Firm attorneys typically bill clients by the hour and track their time in six-minute increments. Firms will require associates to bill a minimum number of hours each year, with additional billable hours potentially leading to bonus payments. On top of billable hours, associates should expect to invest significant time in administrative duties and continuing legal education.

Starting law firm salaries are easiest to identify for large firms through the National Association for Law Placement.[1] Since approximately 2007, annual starting salaries at top law firms in large cities have held steady at $160,000.[2] Starting salaries for large firms in smaller markets range from $100,000 on up.[3] Salaries are less at midsize and small firms, ranging from $40,000 to the low six figures. Although applying for any job is a competitive process, it is important to note that only truly exceptional students are hired by the largest firms, typically after being a summer associate at the firm.

Large firms increasingly are recruiting "lateral hires" to join the firm. These are individuals often with two to three years' experience at another firm. Hiring criteria for these attorneys revolve less around school and class rank and more on the type and quality of experience the attorney has developed in his or her career.

Large Firms

There are many benefits to working for a large firm. The largest firms in the United States employ many attorneys at all levels and often have offices

---

1. NALP, DIRECTORY OF LEGAL EMPLOYERS, http://www.nalpdirectory.com/ (last visited Mar. 24, 2014).

2. Press Release, NALP, Associate Salaries Bobble But Remain Essentially Flat (Sept. 18, 2013), *available at* http://www.nalp.org/uploads/PressReleases/2013ASSRPressRelease.pdf.

3. *Id.*

throughout the country and the world. Large firms bring in large clients and handle big cases and complex transactions that often involve many attorneys. Examples of health care clients represented by large firms include international pharmaceutical companies, multifacility health care organizations, large insurance companies, and trade associations. Typical work done could range from advising on pharmaceutical drug trials and FDA approval of new drugs to complex acquisitions of new facilities and health care groups. The structure of large firms, often with two tiers of partners and senior, mid-level, and new associates, offers attorneys a chance to work within teams and receive mentoring and guidance from senior attorneys.

In deciding the size of a law firm that appeals to you, consider that at a big firm it is likely you will have the opportunity to learn from some of the most renowned attorneys while investing many hours on a specialized portion of big cases or projects. New associates in any large firm often spend their days performing research, due diligence, and document review, among other tasks. Large firms often set high minimum billable hours but, as just discussed, pay the highest starting salaries.

A consequence of working in an office with many attorneys is that attorneys commonly specialize in a particular subset of an area of law. The general breakdown within health law has always been between transactional and regulatory work, although even within these two broad categories subspecialties have developed. For example, a Washington, D.C. office of a top-50 law firm, with over 1,000 attorneys, was recently looking for a mid-level associate to join its health law group in order to focus on Medicare Part D alone. Such specialization can lead to great expertise and value. On the other hand, young associates sometimes express frustration with having assignments that are narrow in scope. That said, the trend toward specialization in large firms is clear and, given their generally higher fee structure and sophisticated range of clients, irreversible.

CAREER PROFILE

Doug Swill
Managing Partner and Chair of the Health Care Practice Group
Drinker Biddle & Reath

I have practiced as a regulatory and transactional health care attorney since 1990. For the last 20 years I have practiced in the national health care group of Drinker Biddle & Reath LLP, a 650-lawyer firm with 12 offices in the United States, including Chicago, where I reside. My career path began following law school graduation from Washington University in St. Louis in 1989. Actually, it was during my final semester as a third-year law student that I discovered a "passion" for health care law during a health law symposium class. Given this rather late discovery, my job search quickly became more challenging. Although I interviewed at several midsize to large firms with health care practices, none offered me a position. At that point, I found an opportunity to both study and serve as a fellow at Loyola University Chicago School of Law's Health Law LLM program.

For the 1989–1990 academic year, I took classes ranging from Medicare/Medicaid to Health Care Finance and interned at the Northwestern Memorial Hospital legal department and the American Medical Association health law department. The year was thrilling and full of great learning and networking experiences, which was helpful for a newcomer to Chicago (from Long Island, New York). One of the most influential mentors of my legal studies and career was Professor John Blum, the first director of the Health Law LLM program at Loyola. Another influential mentor at the time was Ed Bryant, an adjunct professor at Loyola. The academic experience at Loyola served me very well as I look back over the last 23 years.

After receiving my LLM in Health Law degree from Loyola in 1990, I accepted a position as an Assistant State's Attorney for Cook County, where I was dedicated to Cook County Hospital (now known as John Stroger Hospital). I provided both regulatory and transactional support to the hospital's management team as well as to other county officials related to county health care matters. My services ranged from providing advice concerning medical staff matters to addressing issues related to opening Provident Hospital, another county hospital. I was part of a small group of attorneys within the Civil Actions Bureau, located at the Daley Center in downtown Chicago. The bureau had approximately 100 lawyers in various areas and operated in many ways, as I would learn later, like a large law firm. I had many fine mentors with the bureau, including Elizabeth Reidy and Randy Johnston. Additionally, I had the opportunity to practice within the federal litigation group of the bureau, which I welcomed given that health care has a significant federal role, especially under Medicare and Medicaid. This opportunity allowed me to present oral arguments before the Seventh Circuit Court of Appeals in two cases, which was fascinating and a great experience.

After two and a half years of wonderful experiences at the State's Attorney's Office, I considered my next move following a phone call from a legal recruiter. The legal recruiter, who had gotten my name from a fellow assistant state's attorney, told me that a few Chicago law firms were in search of associates for their health care groups. I interviewed with three firms. One of the firms, Gardner Carton & Douglas, stood out for both its national health care practice as well as its civility and camaraderie among attorneys—something I enjoyed at the State's Attorney's Office. I joined as a third-year associate. Looking back, and knowing what I know now about associate development and partner track advancement, it was helpful to "negotiate" being placed as a third-year associate.

When I joined GCD in 1993, or GarCar as it was also known, the firm was based in Chicago with approximately 180 attorneys. GCD also had a Washington, D.C., office, which had approximately 35 attorneys. The health care group had about 17 attorneys, which was considered sizable in the early 1990s, and about a third of the group resided in our D.C. office. We also had litigators and employee benefits attorneys at the firm who were spending a considerable amount of their professional time with our health system clients. Back then and to this day, the largest sector of our health care clients is not-for-profit health care systems that range from large academic medical centers to critical access hospitals. One of the highlights of my practice is representing nonprofit providers, given their mission and governance structure.

As a junior associate in 1993, I was fortunate to be in a fairly busy national health care practice that only had four associates. I was staffed on diligence assignments related to health system affiliations, research, and writing memoranda on the federal Anti-Kickback law and tax-exemption law as well as drafting physician agreements for hospitals. My rolling 12 months billable hour rate was 2,100, and that remained fairly steady for the next eight or so years. The mid-1990s and following was a great time to be an associate in a national health care practice, as I was deployed to many parts of the state and country to work on diligence assignments related to affiliations. These experiences taught me much about health system operations and local market dynamics and afforded me opportunities to meet many health care executives. I also provided outside general counsel services to Children's Memorial Hospital in Chicago (now Lurie Children's) as well as a few other health care institutional clients of the firm. Through the outside general counsel services as well as the affiliation

Continued

transactions I learned how important being part of a larger law firm with multiple departments is to our health care group given the widespread needs of the health system clients.

I became a partner in 1998 and quickly learned the difference between income and equity partner. I didn't care, however, that I was an income partner, as I was thrilled to be made a partner in such a prestigious health care practice as GCD. My first large health system client engaged us in 1999 and is still a client today. A lot has changed since I became a partner in 1998, however. Between 2005 and 2006, GCD began to experience certain "growth" issues that led a few of our partners within the group to leave, which impacted me as one was a mentor to me. However, GCD leadership persevered and found a strategic partner in Drinker Biddle & Reath LLP, based in Philadelphia. Although DBR did not have a sizable health care group as GCD did, the firm did offer a larger platform in terms of additional offices and lawyers in other specialties that could assist our health system clients. More importantly, DBR had a wonderful culture that closely matched that of the "old" GCD, which was an attraction to me when I was choosing law firms to join.

Today DBR has approximately 650 lawyers in 13 offices. We have approximately 35 lawyers in our national health care group, which I chair, and about 125 in total who are members of our health care industry team. About 15 percent of my time is administrative in my role as chair of the group and also as a member of the management committee. For the last decade I have counseled health systems on numerous affiliations and acquisitions, working closely with boards of directors, management, and medical staff leaders. I also provide regulatory compliance advice to many provider clients. The interdisciplinary nature of representing our health industry clients necessitates that I work with many lawyers throughout the firm and, given our engaging culture and dedicated staff, I am thrilled to practice and be part of the management team at DBR.

CAREER PROFILE

Laura Morgan
Associate
McDermott Will & Emery LLP

I am an associate in the Health Industry Advisory Practice Group (HIAPG) at McDermott Will & Emery LLP (McDermott) in the firm's Chicago office. I began as an associate in the fall of 2012 after graduating from Loyola University Chicago School of Law with a Juris Doctor and Certificate in Health Law. As a junior associate in the HIAPG at McDermott, I have had opportunities to take on sophisticated and challenging projects in both the transactional and regulatory areas of health care law.

McDermott has one of the country's largest and most prestigious health care practices, having served health care industry clients for over 30 years. These clients include health care systems, hospitals, physician groups, physician practice management companies, medical device manufacturers, pharmaceutical companies, health insurance companies, and private equity firms investing in the health care field. HIAPG lawyers practice in nearly all areas of health law (with the exception of medical malpractice), including mergers and acquisitions, antitrust, tax exemption, managed care, employee benefits, health information privacy, and Medicare and Medicaid fraud, abuse, and reimbursement issues. There are over 90 HIAPG professionals in McDermott's offices in the United States and around the world with a wealth of experience in these areas, including several non-attorney professionals who assist us with advising clients in the health space. The practice's capabilities are enhanced by the legal experience and skills represented by the firm's approximately 1,000 lawyers in other specialty practice areas internationally. Such a deep bench of experience and expertise enables the HIAPG to provide an unparalleled level of service to our health care industry clients.

I have personally enjoyed working in the health law practice of a large firm because, as a junior associate, I have been trained and mentored by some of the best lawyers in the health law field. Due to its size, reputation, and expertise, the HIAPG has a great variety of cutting-edge work. My colleagues are incredibly intelligent and professional and handle sophisticated and challenging work—work in which I was able to participate even as a first-year associate. I also appreciate having access to an excellent support staff of paralegals and administrative assistants, as well as on-site document production and copy center services, all of which enhance the level of service we are able to provide to our clients. Finally, McDermott

Continued

CAREER PROFILE *Continued*

has a robust pro bono program and encourages all of its attorneys to participate in pro bono work both within and outside of their practice areas.

I have been able to complete a great variety of work in the regulatory and transactional areas of the HIAPG. On the transactional side, I have worked closely with HIAPG transaction teams for hospital and private equity client acquisitions of health care entities and sales of physician practices. I have conducted due diligence, drafted transaction documents and due diligence executive summaries, revised disclosure schedules, and compiled closing documents.

In the last several months, my practice has focused primarily on health care regulatory work for large health care system, hospital, and physician practice management clients in the areas of compliance with the federal physician self-referral law (known as the Stark law), the Anti-Kickback Statute, and state corporate practice of medicine regulations. I have worked closely with a McDermott partner in assisting clients with identifying and addressing physician compensation arrangements that potentially implicate the Stark law, including disclosing and resolving such matters with the Department of Justice and the Centers for Medicare and Medicaid Services. I have also been involved in assisting clients with audits of their physician practices to determine their compliance with the Stark law's in-office ancillary services exception, and I have assisted clients with comprehensive physician employment contract remediation projects through development of template employment agreements and replacement of or revisions to potentially problematic agreements.

I particularly enjoy health care regulatory work because of the challenge in learning a complex area of the law and the satisfaction in being an asset to a client seeking to understand and comply with the applicable requirements. I have found that regulatory projects, such as the ones just described, typically require regular communication with clients over a long period, which has provided me with institutional knowledge about their operations, activities, goals, and objectives and which I have found to be personally and professionally rewarding.

Finally, through my pro bono work, I have developed corporate drafting skills (e.g., drafting organizational documents for not-for-profit organizations) and have worked in areas beyond my legal "comfort zone" (e.g., preparing and submitting applications for asylum and withholding of removal for individuals seeking asylum before the Department of Homeland Security). It has been deeply satisfying to have the opportunity to use my legal skills to assist clients who do not have the ability to pay for legal services, and I have gained unique skills and insights through this work that I have been able to use in serving clients within the health care industry.

Midsize Firms

Midsize firms offer some of the same features as larger ones, but with some differences. Many midsize firms also have offices in different parts of the country and occasionally operate internationally. These firms have some large clients and also handle big cases and complex transactions. That said, smaller clients are much more dominant in a midsize firm than in a larger practice setting. Fees typically are lower in midsize firms, allowing them to compete for smaller clients than do their larger brethren. Typical health care industry clients for a midsize firm might include smaller, more specialized pharmaceutical and medical device companies, physician groups, and midsize health care organizations. Their structure often mimics that of larger firms, with tiered partnerships and senior, mid-level, and new associates.

Cases/projects at midsize firms are normally staffed more leanly than at larger firms, meaning attorneys still work in teams but likely with fewer members. This arrangement can offer younger associates great opportunities to become more involved in a particular matter while still receiving mentoring and guidance from senior attorneys. New attorneys at midsize firms may find themselves having more routine access to and interaction with senior partners than might those at larger firms. On the other hand, depending upon the capabilities of the firm, the ability to specialize in health law, or within health law, may be limited. Midsize firms typically set high billable hour requirements, although often not quite as high as those of larger firms, and pay starting salaries below the large firm average.

CAREER PROFILE

Kimberly Boike
Partner
Chuhak & Tecson PC

Chuhak & Tecson PC is a midsize law firm located in Chicago, Illinois. We currently have approximately 70 attorneys working in the following practice areas: aviation litigation and transactions; banking; condominium and common interest community associations; corporate transactions and business law; employment; estate and trust administration and litigation; estate planning and asset protection; healthcare; litigation; not-for-profit

Continued

CAREER PROFILE *Continued*

and mission-based organizations; real estate; and tax and employee benefits. I concentrate my practice in the areas of corporate health care law and not-for-profit law.

I have worked at Chuhak & Tecson PC since my second year of law school, as part of the firm's law clerk program. As a law clerk, I assisted attorneys across the firm's various practice areas on matters ranging from researching complex health care issues to drafting litigation briefs. This broad range of experience allowed me to gain exposure to virtually every practice area and enabled me to make an informed decision about the area of law in which I wanted to practice. As a result of my law clerk experience, I decided to focus my legal career in the corporate health care and not-for-profit fields. I was hired by Chuhak & Tecson PC as an associate in the corporate health care group following law school and was recently elevated to principal.

As a member of the corporate health care group, I focus my practice on advising health care providers across the spectrum of the health care industry on a multitude of issues. For hospitals and health systems, I work on complex compliance issues such as structuring relationships to be compliant with federal and state health care laws, including the Stark law, fraud and abuse laws, and the Civil Monetary Penalty law. I have also advised hospitals and health systems on disclosures under the Stark Self-Disclosure Protocol. In addition, I work closely with our hospital and health system clients to strategize and implement compliance policies as well as to enhance their understanding of potential risk areas to avoid future compliance issues. Further, in addition to compliance issues, I regularly work with hospitals and health systems on medical staff issues, including credentialing issues and medical staff disciplinary issues.

In addition to hospitals and health systems, I work with continuing care retirement communities to advise them on legal aspects across the continuum of care they provide to their residents, including independent living, assisted living, skilled care, and home health care. I counsel our continuing care clients on concerns related to life safety code issues, health survey issues, obtaining tax-exempt bond financing, revising admissions procedures, drafting affiliation agreements, and facilitating mergers and acquisitions. I routinely work with hospitals, health systems, and continuing care retirement communities that are sponsored by religious groups. As a result, I have extensive experience in working through unique legal issues associated with such religious sponsors in carrying out their health care ministries across the continuum of care.

With respect to physicians, I work with individual physicians and physician practices of all sizes to advise them on all aspects of their business, including negotiating their first employment agreements, structuring partnership buy-ins in a tax efficient manner, negotiating partnership agreements, structuring buy-sell agreements, and advising on compliance issues such as HIPAA.

A few years ago, I helped to found Chuhak & Tecson PC's not-for-profit practice group, which is devoted to serving the unique needs of not-for-profit organizations. While many of the hospitals, health systems, and continuing care retirement communities that I work with are nonprofit organizations, I also work with not-for-profit organizations of all sizes outside the health care field, including child care organizations, food pantries, churches, family foundations, associations, and chambers of commerce. I work with our not-for-profit clients on issues including corporate restructuring, obtaining and maintaining tax-exempt status, governance issues, affiliations, and executive compensation matters.

I am also one of the founding members of Chuhak & Tecson PC's Women Helping Women initiative, which is an invitation-only, after-hours networking group that integrates business development with philanthropy. Designed exclusively by the women at Chuhak & Tecson PC, we host biannual mixer events, which bring together local women business leaders, entrepreneurs, and strategic partners—weaving networking, business development, and community service into a single event that benefits not only the attendees but our community as well.

One of the things I enjoy most about working in a midsize firm is the emphasis that is placed on educating our clients and potential clients on issues that are important to them. I have always been passionate about education and Chuhak & Tecson PC has given me the opportunity to continuously be in front of our clients and potential clients in an educational setting to work on issues that impact their business. I have worked extensively on educating residents and fellows nationally about issues related to the business of medicine. I have recently spoken to residency programs of the Duke University School of Medicine in North Carolina and the Morehouse School of Medicine in Georgia. I find it incredibly fulfilling to work with residents and fellows on issues relating to the business side of their future practices so that they are prepared for their careers not only from a clinical perspective but from a business perspective as well.

In addition to my educational work with physicians, I work on educating not-for-profit board members and senior management on governance issues. These educational sessions focus on the role of board members, their relationship to the chief executive officer, and the implementation of a board strategy designed around strategic governance. The goal of such educational sessions is to provide members of the board a clear understanding of their roles as board members, so that their time serving on the board is used as effectively and efficiently as possible. In addition to governance

Continued

CAREER PROFILE *Continued*

issues, I work on educating boards of directors on succession planning for both the board and senior management and on fund-raising issues.

Another part of my position that I truly enjoy is meeting with our clients at their place of business to gain an understanding of the operational aspects of their business. My goal is to have my clients view me as a strategic partner and not just a legal technician. By understanding my clients' businesses, I know how legal issues I am working on will impact them from an operational perspective, and I can design a strategy that will work effectively with their business.

Small Firms

Unlike in large firms, new attorneys at smaller law firms are often given broader responsibility, albeit for smaller matters. Small firms typically handle smaller clients and transactions and cases that are smaller in scope. Typical clients handled by small firms include physician groups and individual physicians, individuals involved in medical malpractice cases, and insurance coverage disputes. Cases and projects are staffed with fewer attorneys, meaning young associates may be paired with just one or two senior attorneys on a matter.

At smaller firms, a new attorney is likely to be assigned client cases in which he or she will have the opportunity to speak frequently with the client and opposing counsel and will be pushed to address new areas of the law as they arise relative to the client. Such responsibility can empower the associate to see the big picture and offer valuable client contact. Smaller firms generally require the fewest billable hours but also generally pay lower salaries than larger firms.

Boutique Firms

The number of boutique health law firms is increasing. Boutique law firms often have developed very specialized niches, such as elder law, behavioral health, physician contracts, and health planning/licensure issues. Still others will have a "general" health law practice. These firms offer attorneys interested in health law the unique opportunity to work only for health law clients primarily on health law issues. The size and structure of boutique firms vary, as do their pay rates and billable hours requirements. Boutique firms do provide excellent opportunities for mentoring new attorneys in the field, as partners and senior attorneys at these firms often have extensive experience working for health care clients.

Law Firm Clients

As Chapter 2 details, different practice settings are commonly associated with different substantive areas within health law. In choosing a law firm that is right for you, it is important to consider who you wish to represent, as different law firms represent different individuals and organizations. In general, here are some of the kinds of clients law firms represent in health law matters. Because the health care industry is continuing to rapidly expand and innovate, and because many new types of actors are entering (software companies developing apps, for example), this discussion is by no means exhaustive.

Individual Patients
Some health care attorneys may represent patients. Although medical malpractice (tort) litigation has traditionally not been considered part of health law, this is changing as the instances of patients suing under contract theories expand. Litigation to enforce insurance contracts, secure needed treatment, or discharge medical debt is increasing. As more financial burden is placed on patients to fund their care (through, for example, higher deductibles and coinsurance), attorneys assuming the role of patient advocate are likely to find themselves with an increasing case load.

Individual Health Care Providers
Firms may represent physicians and other health care professionals who are participating in mergers or joint ventures, need help structuring a private practice, wish assistance in general contract/real estate/tax matters, are charged with professional malpractice, are facing disciplinary or licensure actions, or require counsel in a variety of other matters.

Institutional Health Care Providers

Firms often handle various legal matters for institutional health care providers, including hospitals, ambulatory surgery centers, nursing homes, and long-term care facilities, among many others. Attorneys at firms that represent institutional providers assist clients with any legal issues that may arise as a result of operating a complex business in a highly regulated environment, including licensure applications, contracts, drafting and defending policies, interpreting Medicare and third-party insurance, and other regulatory laws and tax matters. A brief sampling of issues includes regulatory matters, medical staff relations, provider termination proceedings, managed care and other third-party contract issues, corporate restructurings, acquisitions and mergers, and compliance programs.

Insurance Companies

Health insurance companies—payors—are a major component of the health care industry. As complex organizations they raise a host of corporate, regulatory, and litigation issues. Further, as payors and providers begin working together in close relationships, work associated with insurance companies is likely to expand significantly.

Pharmaceuticals, Suppliers, and Vendors

The pharmaceutical sector is one of the fastest growing components of the health care industry. In part this is due to the phenomenal expansion of technology within the drug development architecture as well as the rapidly increasing sophistication of genomics. Legal issues arising within the industry range from issues of regulation—food and drug safety, clinical research, privacy/data security—to reimbursement, intellectual property, and corporate and transactional work.

Suppliers and vendors are also a crucial component of organizations working with health care. Companies that produce medical supplies and equipment, offer services (from laundry to cafeteria to supply chain to management, etc.), and provide ancillary services (outside laboratory testing, blood banks) raise issues unique to themselves along with an added layer of complexity given the patient care and safety issues inherent in health care.

Trade Associations

Firms also handle matters for the many health care trade associations. Given the many unique perspectives inherent in health care, the industry is rife with membership associations ranging from the very large (American Medical Association and American Hospital Association) to smaller specialty groups. Law firms representing trade associations that are involved in policy work may review or propose draft legislation and write amicus briefs. They may develop policy papers, lobby, or otherwise advocate for their clients, including providing direct representation in litigation. Trade associations often have complex corporate structures, and law firms assist with corporate governance matters. Law firms also assist with antitrust and tax issues, employment agreements, regulatory and compliance matters, credentialing, publishing, and intellectual property, among a myriad of other issues that can arise.

Government

Federal, state, and local governments all play an important role in regulating health care. Agencies at each level employ attorneys in areas related to public health and health care delivery. There are many opportunities to practice health law within government organizations at the federal, state, and municipal levels. These positions generally give new attorneys early hands-on experience. The following descriptions include the agencies best known for legal work in and related to health care. Agencies vary by state and local government, and those seeking to work at these types of agencies are encouraged to investigate further those in the geographic areas they are interested in.

Federal Government

The federal government regulates health care through a number of agencies and departments.

U.S. Department of Health and Human Services

The Department of Health and Human Services (HHS) serves as the U.S. government's principal agency for protecting the health of all Americans and providing essential human services, especially for those who are least able to help themselves. There are a number of operating divisions within HHS that employ health care attorneys. Some of the key divisions are described in the following list. A full list of HHS divisions is available on the agency's website.[4] While most HHS divisions operate in Washington, D.C., and Maryland, there are also ten regional offices throughout the United States that employ attorneys.[5]

- *Office of the General Counsel.* The Office of the General Counsel serves as the lead legal office for HHS. This division employs a number of attorneys to ensure that HHS divisions operate within the bounds of the laws and authority that govern them.
- *Office for Civil Rights.* The Office for Civil Rights (OCR) enforces federal laws that prohibit discrimination by health care providers receiving funding from the federal government. Attorneys working for the OCR often investigate and represent HHS in claims involving discrimination in the provision of services and privacy and security of health information.
- *Agency for Healthcare Research and Quality.* The Agency for Healthcare Research and Quality (AHRQ) is the division of HHS charged with improving the quality, safety, efficiency, and effectiveness of health care across the country. AHRQ supports research to improve health care quality and implement evidence-based decision making. Attorneys in this division may become involved in health policy and regulatory matters.
- *Centers for Disease Control and Prevention.* The Centers for Disease Control and Prevention (CDC) is the division of HHS that responds to health emergencies. The CDC conducts research and investigations

---

4. U.S. DEP'T OF HEALTH & HUMAN SERVS., *Where Can I Work?*, http://www.hhs.gov/careers/where/index.html (last visited Mar. 24, 2014).

5. U.S. DEP'T OF HEALTH & HUMAN SERVS., *HHS Regional Offices*, http://www.hhs.gov/about/regions (last visited Mar. 24, 2014).

designed to prevent and control all health threats, diseases, disabilities, injuries, and workplace hazards. In 2000, the CDC Public Health Law Program was established to improve the health of the public through law. One of the program's strategic goals is to develop legal preparedness of the public health system to address terrorism and other national public health priorities. Attorneys working for the CDC often focus in the public health arena, working in areas including health policy, federalism, patient safety, and privacy.

- *Food and Drug Administration.* The Food and Drug Administration (FDA) is the agency of HHS responsible for regulating food, dietary supplements, drugs, cosmetics, and medical devices. As an administrative agency in the executive branch of the government, the FDA derives all of its authority and jurisdiction from various acts of Congress. The main source of the FDA's authority is the Federal Food, Drug, and Cosmetic Act. Regulatory enforcement is carried out by Consumer Safety Officers within the Office of Regulatory Affairs, and criminal matters are handled by special agents within the Office of Criminal Investigations. Attorneys employed by the FDA represent the agency in investigations regarding clinical drug trials, applications for new drugs and devices, and marketing, among other things.

- *The Centers for Medicare and Medicaid Services.* The Centers for Medicare and Medicaid Services (CMS) is the division of HHS that ensures effective, up-to-date health care coverage, develops and implements reimbursement policy governing health care providers, and promotes quality care for beneficiaries. CMS also operates through regional offices around the country. Attorneys for CMS work in several key areas of health law including, but not limited to, regulation, compliance, health information privacy (HIPAA), quality assurance, and claims resolution. The Centers for Medicare and Medicaid Services' (CMS) Office of Legislation serves as a liaison and resource for the U.S. Congress to explain the polices, payment systems, and operations of Medicare, Medicaid, and the Children's Health Insurance Program (CHIP). The Office of Legislation responds to inquiries from members of Congress and congressional committees. This office provides another place for attorneys to work on regulation, compliance, and policy matters.

- *Office of Inspector General.* Under Public Law 95-452, the Office of Inspector General (OIG) must protect the integrity of the Department of Health and Human Services programs and the health and welfare of beneficiaries of those programs. The OIG uses a nationwide network of audits, investigations, inspections, and other mission-related functions performed by OIG components to report program and management problems to Congress and the secretary. A particular focus of the office is policing federal health care fraud laws, including physician self-referral. Many attorneys working for OIG represent the agency in investigations involving these matters.

U.S. Department of Justice, Office of the U.S. Attorney General

Several Department of Justice (DOJ) divisions address health care issues, including the Antitrust, Civil, and Criminal Divisions as well as the Office of Diversion Control. Some key divisions dealing with health-related issues are described here.

- *Antitrust Division.* The purpose of the Antitrust Division of the DOJ is to promote and protect the competitive process, as well as the economy in general, through the enforcement of antitrust laws, which apply to all industries, including health care. In addition, this division provides guidance to businesses, including hospitals and other health care facilities, and helps them structure and organize their operations in accordance with the antitrust laws.
- *Civil Division.* The Civil Division is the largest litigation division within the DOJ. It represents the United States, federal agencies and their employees, the president, members of Congress, the federal judiciary, and the citizens of the United States. Its cases often have significant domestic and foreign policy implications. The Civil Division devotes significant resources to investigating and litigating health care fraud, including Medicare and Medicaid fraud. A health law student or lawyer interested in medical malpractice litigation or consumer litigation concerning medical products should look further into this division's consumer protection practice.

- *Criminal Division.* The Criminal Division of the DOJ investigates and enforces all federal criminal laws not specifically assigned to other divisions. Attorneys in this division litigate important cases involving high-level health care fraud and white-collar crime, along with any other matters involving enforcement of federal criminal laws in health care. In addition to litigation, attorneys in this division draft policy regarding enforcement of criminal acts. These attorneys provide legal advice and assistance to federal prosecutors, investigating agencies, the attorney general, both houses of Congress, and the White House.

- *U.S. Department of Justice, United States Attorneys.* The Department of Justice also oversees 94 federal districts, each of which has an appointed United States Attorney to conduct trial work within that district to which the United States is a party. These offices employ many attorneys as federal prosecutors and are often divided into sections similar to those listed earlier for the DOJ. Many cases involve civil and criminal health care matters.

Federal Trade Commission

The Federal Trade Commission (FTC) has the dual charge of protecting consumers and promoting competition. While its sphere of activities goes well beyond health care, the agency does have a significant impact in the health care arena. Traditionally, this focus has been in the antitrust area, with the FTC sharing antitrust enforcement responsibility with the Department of Justice. For example, the FTC's Bureau of Competition receives pre-merger filing notices (Hart-Scott-Rodino filings) along with the DOJ, and can choose to bring an action to stop a proposed merger or acquisition which it deems would harm consumers. In the health care sector, several important cases have been brought by the FTC.

Recently, the FTC has stepped up its enforcement in the privacy area, choosing to investigate and challenge breaches of data privacy and security. This potentially represents a rich area of increased investigations and prosecutions for the agency.

Health law attorneys would be able to work on a variety of investigatory and enforcement activities within the agency. The specialized knowledge that they bring would be a strong benefit to a legal counsel position.

Office of Diversion Control

The Drug Enforcement Administration's (DEA) Office of Diversion Control is responsible for policing the diversion of controlled pharmaceuticals and controlled chemicals. This office coordinates investigations, drafts legislation and regulations, establishes national drug production quotas, controls the importation and exportation of drugs and chemicals, and monitors and tracks the distribution of certain controlled substances. Attorneys working here would become involved in all facets of the office's work.

Internal Revenue Service

A bureau of the Department of the Treasury, the Internal Revenue Service (IRS) is the U.S. government agency that collects taxes and enforces the internal revenue laws. Since the majority of hospitals and many skilled nursing facilities and elder care and home care providers are exempt from taxation, the IRS polices these organizations in regard to their tax-exempt status. Attorneys here require special health law expertise to understand the impact of federal tax law/policy on health care providers.

U.S. Department of Labor

The U.S. Department of Labor (DOL) is a cabinet department of the government responsible for occupational safety, wage and hour standards, unemployment insurance benefits, re-employment services, and some economic statistics. Many state governments also have such departments. The DOL's purposes are to foster, promote, and develop the welfare of working people, to improve their working conditions, and to enhance their opportunities for profitable employment. Health care is a very labor-intensive enterprise, and hence expertise in health law is important for DOL attorneys concentrating in the health care arena. Attorneys working in the Occupational Safety and Health Administration, an agency within the DOL, often require an in-depth knowledge of health care law.

Social Security Administration

The U.S. Social Security Administration (SSA) administers the country's social insurance program. Attorneys are employed in several areas, including the Office of the General Counsel, which advises the SSA on all legal matters. Additionally, many attorneys work for the Office of Disability Adjudication and Review, administering the review and appeals process for Social Security benefits.

Department of Veterans Affairs

The U.S. Department of Veterans Affairs (VA) operates the nation's largest integrated health system, providing health services to over 8 million veterans through the Veterans Health Administration. The VA oversees health benefits for veterans and operates a system of hospitals and clinics at which veterans receive care. Health law attorneys provide the same panoply of services within the VA as do their private sector counterparts, including advising on issues ranging from patient care to regulatory matters.

Searching for Jobs in the U.S. Government

The U.S. government posts all job openings to, and requires all applications to be routed through, its employment site: www.usajobs.com. This is the best starting point for viewing open positions. Additionally, job seekers might find some of the following resources helpful.

- For students seeking federal government internships, Go Government is a site sponsored by the Partnership for Public Service: http://gogovernment.org/
- The Federal Jobs Digest is a publication featuring all open government positions. This publication offers online and print editions: www.jobsfed.com
- GovtJobs.com is a website featuring open federal and state government positions: www.govtjobs.com

State Government

Each state operates agencies that are involved in the regulation and administration of health care. While the number and names of agencies vary by state,[6] there are some common types of agencies that employ attorneys.

---

6. Health Access, *Government Agencies*, http://www.health-access.org/item.asp?id=123 (last visited Mar. 24, 2014).

Attorney General

The main agency responsible for enforcing state laws related to the provision of health care is the attorney general.

- *Health Care Fraud or Consumer Protection Division.* Most states have departments designed to enforce health care laws that protect consumers. These laws prevent fraud in the sale and delivery of health care products and services. Attorneys here will lead investigations and litigate matters involving serious violations of law.
- *Medicaid Fraud Unit.* Nearly every state has a division of the state attorney general's office that prosecutes criminal and civil actions involving provider fraud and fraud in the administration of the state's Medicaid program. Sometimes these are organized into criminal and civil divisions. Although these units are part of the Office of the Attorney General of most states, they may also operate as separate agencies or as parts of other state agencies or law enforcement authorities.
- *Health Care Mediation Division.* Some states operate divisions that provide mediation and alternative dispute resolution for all parties involved in health care disputes.

Department of Public Health

Although they have different names and varying responsibilities, all states have a department of public health, which generally promotes the health of the people of the state through the prevention and control of disease and injury. Many state health departments provide various services, including vaccinations; food, water, and drug safety testing; infectious disease control; and the collection and evaluation of health statistics to develop prevention and regulatory programs. Some state health departments are also responsible for social services. Some departments of public health also provide licensure to hospitals, nursing homes, and other care sites or providers. Attorneys here may advise on everything from health policy through enforcement actions.

Department of Insurance

State departments of insurance protect the rights of state citizens by advancing a competitive insurance market, regulating and monitoring the insurance market, and providing information and assistance to consumers. More specifically, the departments overseeing consumer health insurance assist consumers in their health issues by explaining patients' rights and coverage provisions and by further handling citizens' problems and complaints. Many state departments of insurance also provide services specifically to seniors by training volunteers to counsel seniors about Medicare and Medicaid supplement and long-term insurance. Attorneys here are skilled in the intricacies of insurance law and their impact on consumers, patients, and providers.

Insurance Exchanges

With the implementation of the PPACA's required health care insurance exchanges, many states also now operate their own insurance exchanges or operate an exchange in cooperation with the federal government. States have handled administration of exchanges differently, but some have developed departments or agencies tasked with oversight of the exchange marketplaces. Attorneys are key players in exchange-centered agencies and departments because there are a number of statutes and regulations to consider in operating an exchange.

Department of Health Care

Each state has a department that administers Medicaid and other federal benefits programs to citizens within the state. In some states the departments or agencies that administer benefits programs for health care also administer other family benefits programs and oversee family and child services. Attorneys here become involved in matters of health policy and program administration.

Department of Veterans Affairs

Departments of veterans affairs operate within most states to provide care to veterans. Most often, these services are supplemental to the federal VA benefits. They vary by state but can include health care education, employment, housing, and other assistance.

Health Care Licensing Boards and Agencies

Each state regulates individual health care providers within its borders. This includes licensing doctors, nurses, and other types of approved providers within the state. These boards also oversee disciplinary matters, including investigation of complaints and suspension or revocation of licensure. Attorneys working in this area often are involved in investigations of licensing violations as well as administrative hearings to prosecute licensing violations.

Local Government

Many municipal and county governments are also involved in the provision of health services. The National Association of County and City Health Officials (NACCHO) provides a helpful overview of the types of jobs in health law and policy offered on the local level.[7]

County Boards

Many counties are governed by boards or commissions that oversee provision of services within the county. In some areas, this includes the provision of health care and oversight of public health services.

Public Health Departments

Many counties and cities have separate public health departments to provide public health services on a local level. They perform many of the same functions as, and often work in conjunction with, state agencies.

City Legal Departments

Legal jobs in city departments vary widely. City legal offices vary in size and structure depending on the size of the city. These departments are overseen in some cities by an elected attorney and in others by appointed officials. They perform a variety of criminal and civil work. Cities of a size to require in-house health care attorneys often have sizable public hospitals or skilled nursing facilities operated by the city. These attorneys perform

---

7. NAT'L ASS'N OF COUNTY AND CITY HEALTH OFFICIALS, http://www.naccho.org (last visited Mar. 24, 2014).

typical general counsel functions, with an eye to the special enabling laws governing the city institution(s).

Searching for Jobs in State and Local Government

Because the structures of state and local governments vary widely, job searches should be tailored to specific areas. Attorneys interested in working in health care law and policy for local and state governments should familiarize themselves with the agencies and their organizational structure in their geographic areas of interest. Local networking is essential to understanding the structure of agencies and the key officials in the area.

CAREER PROFILE

Shawn Mathis
Staff Attorney
Legislative Council Service, State of New Mexico

The Legislative Council Service is the drafting, legal, and research staff for the New Mexico legislature. The Council Service serves all members of the legislature without regard to political affiliation, seniority, or leadership position. The staff also drafts legislation for executive and judicial agencies. By statute, staff may not disclose the contents or nature of any request or statement for service without the consent of the legislator for whom the work is done.

As a legislative staff attorney, I often work long hours in a very interesting and demanding environment, with primary responsibility for health policy. This broad subject area encompasses topics such as physical and behavioral health programs and policies; programs for persons with developmental disabilities; state and federal health care programs; state licensure and oversight of health care professionals and facilities; health disparities among segments of the state's population; relationships between the state and tribal governments that impact health care for Native Americans; rural health care challenges; the health care workforce shortage; telemedicine; the state's health information exchange; health care research and programs conducted by the state's universities; the education of health care professionals by various state institutions of higher education; substance use and abuse; scope of practice; regulation of health insurance by the state; Medicaid expansion, the health insurance exchange, and other aspects of the federal Patient Protection and Affordable Care Act; public health issues and tracking; health care privacy; guardianship; advance

Continued

CAREER PROFILE *Continued*

directives and laws regarding end-of-life decisions; abortion; teen pregnancy; medical marijuana; prescription drug abuse; long-term care and aging; medical malpractice laws; and tort reform.

At the request of a legislator, staff attorneys perform legal research and prepare non-campaign materials such as letters, speeches, talking points, and op-ed pieces. We also field calls from constituents who have questions or who might need help resolving problems. New Mexico has one legislative session each year, alternating between 30-day and 60-day legislative sessions. During session, staff attorneys work around the clock, drafting, amending, and substituting bills. On occasion, staff attorneys are asked to explain proposed legislation to the legislative committees through which a bill must pass to get to a vote on the floor.

Drafting legislation requires a unique skill set of attention to detail, organization, and clarity in the written word. To ensure statutory uniformity, one must adhere to strict drafting conventions and standardized language specific to New Mexico. While bills might be based upon legislation from another state or upon drafts proposed by a lobbyist or legislator, the staff attorney's job is to draft a bill that meets New Mexico's formal requirements and that is faithful to the legislator's idea. Although a staff attorney is prohibited from advocating for specific legislation, the attorney may suggest different formats or approaches to accomplish the bill sponsor's legislative goal. As part of the bill-drafting process, research is often required to determine whether proposed legislation would be constitutional under both the state and federal constitutions and to ensure that defined terms or provisions within a proposed bill do not inadvertently conflict with existing state and, often, federal laws. After bills are introduced, they go through committees and are often amended or substituted, with staff attorneys making these changes as required, also according to a strict drafting process.

When the legislature is not in session, interim legislative committees meet several times during the summer and fall, often in smaller communities throughout the state. These committee meetings are educational, similar to a conference or seminar, providing legislators with the opportunity to question presenters and to hear from constituents during the public comment segment. I have staffed the Legislative Health and Human Services Committee and its Behavioral Health and Disabilities Concerns subcommittees, as well as the Tobacco Settlement Revenue Oversight Committee. The staff attorney assigned to a committee drafts the committee work plan, which sets forth the topics that will be on the committee's agenda during the interim, under the direction of the committee chairs. The staff attorney identifies and schedules presenters on the topics selected for the work plan. These presenters may include representatives of federal, state, tribal, or local agencies, boards, or institutions; advocacy groups; academic institutions; trade or professional organizations; or providers such as hospitals, community health care agencies, or physicians and other licensed health care professionals. In addition, the staff attorney is responsible for the committee agenda, minutes, and posting of meeting materials on the legislature's website. The staff attorney also prepares a final interim committee report.

In 2010, I made a strategic career decision to pursue a specialization in health law to build upon my previous experience representing clients in other highly regulated industries. I have found that my background as a litigator and in the private sector has proven invaluable when providing legal advice to legislators or when drafting legislation.

In-House

Large companies, such as hospitals, senior service "chains," pharmaceutical and device manufacturers, and insurance companies, frequently have an office of general counsel where in-house attorneys review company policies and practices. In-house counsel often utilize outside counsel from law firms for specialized matters, such as specialized regulatory needs, litigation matters, and complex transactions. In-house counsel handle employment and routine transactional, contract, litigation, and compliance matters. Pharmaceutical and device manufacturers often have in-house attorneys who specialize in intellectual property.

In-house lawyers work for a single company, entity, or group of entities, providing advice on legal matters related to business activities. These matters range from government regulations to contracts with other companies to agreements with labor unions. Typically, lawyers work for three or more years in law firms before being considered for in-house positions. Salaries for in-house positions vary widely depending on the size and location of the organization and the complexity of the legal work involved. The following are a few examples of the different entities for which in-house health law attorneys may work.

Health Care Providers

Health care providers hire attorneys in a number of capacities. Attorneys may be hired in the office of the general counsel. These attorneys represent the organization and provide advice on a variety of matters, from licensure to patient care to litigation oversight and general corporate and transactional matters. Attorneys are increasingly being hired in compliance departments. Compliance is tasked with developing policies and procedures to ensure that the organization is compliant with governing regulations. Compliance departments often spend a significant amount of time on employee and medical staff education.

Attorneys, especially those with a clinical background, may also be hired in the risk management department. Risk management is responsible for working within the organization to promote patient safety and assist in investigating violations of same. Finally, sophisticated organizations may employ health care attorneys in a variety of other areas depending upon needs, such as human relations, physician recruiting, and any number of areas where business and legal issues brush up against each other and a specialized legal background might be helpful. To locate health care providers throughout the United States, check http://www.hospitalconnectsearch.com/.

CAREER PROFILE

Nancy Paridy
Senior Vice President, General Counsel, and
Government Affairs/Corporate Secretary
Rehabilitation Institute of Chicago

Don't tell anyone, but I have the absolute best job on earth! As Senior Vice President, General Counsel, and Government Affairs/Corporate Secretary of the Rehabilitation Institute of Chicago, I am in the unique position of collaborating with individuals from all walks of life, working together to solve complex medical, ethical, and legal issues; to anticipate, predict, and facilitate resolutions for future problems (some of which no one even knows exist); and to develop relationships between companies ensuring the purpose of the organization is met, all while attempting to engender a strong cultural match. I can honestly say that I never have a dull day. Likewise, I can also say that there is never a day I don't learn something new! There is never a day that I wonder why I went into the law!

The springboard for my widely varied role was my desire to be both a trial lawyer and a corporate lawyer—a rare breed in this world. I have always enjoyed being the outlier from a traditional path; thus, the combination has suited me very well. As a litigator, you must be armed with a myriad of skills ranging from thinking on your feet before a potentially intimidating judge to feeling empathy for a troubled client to being able to describe a situation to someone who has never had any training—or interest—in a field. As a corporate attorney, you must learn to cross every "t" and dot every "i" while creating a flawless document that will capture every anticipated development in a relationship. You must also have the judgment to know when to walk away from the deal without letting personal feelings get in the way. Once you combine all those traits, you are on the way to becoming a right hand to any chief executive officer of an organization, an instrumental advisor to the board, and a beacon of transparency and honesty for the employees of your company.

How did I get to where I am today? It is due to a lot of help from my friends and a drive to constantly improve in a career that would challenge me. Growing up, I initially thought I would be a teacher, but when I got to college I wanted to pursue medicine or law. Because of a wonderful mentor and college professor, Sterling Kernek, and Joseph Bartylak, a friend and founder of the Land of Lincoln Legal Assistance Foundation, I headed into the legal field. In 1983, the year that I passed the bar in the state of Illinois, I chose Chicago as my home of choice for my career. Even though I am a dyed-in-the-wool St. Louis Cardinals fan, I moved to Chicago because of the career opportunities in the field of law.

I began my career at Ungaretti and Harris (at the time known as Cofield, Ungaretti, Harris and Slavin [CUHS]). Spawned from Kirkland and Ellis, this was a burgeoning firm that prided itself on the highest quality legal practice while operating in a collegial setting. Mike Coffield, a fabulous mentor, never met a client that he couldn't represent. He taught me that the subject matter could always be learned and that litigation was more art than science. You had to feel comfortable in your own skin and master a subject before you could teach others. Mike saw judges, jurors, and even opposing counsel as students who were interested in learning the topic you knew. It was up to the skilled trial attorney to guide them through teaching to the "right result."

I loved being a new associate at CUHS, as it was fast paced and I was learning firsthand; I had the opportunity to work on the *Amoco Cadiz* matter, which was ultimately argued before the U.S. Supreme Court. The case resulted from a tragic oil spill off the coast of Brittany, France, in 1978. Besides working on the *Cadiz* matter, I was told that I was the youngest woman to argue a case before the Seventh Circuit Court of Appeals and

Continued

to work on a number of securities and corporate matters as well as assist in running the firm's summer associate program. I was also fortunate to be assigned as one of the outside counsel to a number of Cook County Hospital matters. Although medical malpractice was very different from the securities and corporate matters that CUHS routinely handled, it taught me the importance of trial work and litigation. The more time I spent in the courtroom, the more I wanted to be a successful trial attorney. Eventually, I realized that I wanted a more robust daily courtroom practice.

In 1985, I accepted a job offer from Rooks Pitts and Poust, now known as Dykema. However, before I left CUHS, I assisted in the trial of the first medical malpractice case in which a million dollars was offered to the plaintiff. The settlement was rejected, and the case proceeded to trial. We eventually prevailed and obtained a "not guilty" verdict. The morning after the verdict, I announced I was leaving for Dykema. Mike paid me the ultimate professional compliment when he asked me to consult on the appeal of the trial that we had just won while I was practicing at my new law firm.

At Dykema, I was supported in my love of learning and surrounded by colleagues who allowed me to challenge myself further—I decided to pursue my LLM in Health Law. Early on in my practice at Dykema, I enjoyed defending physicians, hospitals, and other health care providers in all types of litigation. Nonetheless, some of my yearnings as a corporate lawyer crept back. I decided to head to Loyola University Chicago, not only because it has one of the most respected health law programs in the country, with an outstanding faculty, but because it focused on the corporate side of being a health care lawyer, which complimented my prior experience as a litigator. Ultimately, I received my LLM in 1988.

In 1990, I became a partner at Rooks Pitts, a truly high-quality firm with a conscience. By then, I had a fabulous practice that combined the best of litigation with a growing corporate health care practice. Although a bit schizophrenic in a law firm setting, the training could not have been better for my current position. While a partner in private practice, I began to realize that I also had a passion for strategy and business development.

When a friend called to ask if I would consider developing a general counsel's office and then mentioned that it was at the Rehabilitation Institute of Chicago (RIC), how could I resist? The Rehabilitation Institute's reputation preceded it; it is currently the number one ranked physical medicine and rehabilitation hospital in the country, a position that it has held for 24 years in a row as ranked by *U.S. News and World Report*. No other hospital in the country has held the number one standing in any field as long as RIC. I could combine my litigation skills with my corporate prowess. I could also act as a confidant to the Board and CEO and be a business leader. Teaching would be a part of what I did each and every day. It was my dream come true!

Almost 20 years ago to the day I am writing this, I joined RIC. I was the first leadership hire who had not grown up in the organization. Virtually every other leader had started as a nurse or a physician or a social worker or therapist. I quickly realized that the more I could be a support, resource, and counselor, I would learn more about the organization and become an essential part of the culture.

I have had numerous experiences over the course of my career at RIC—serving as head of human resources as well as managed care and as its Chief Compliance Officer, assisting in numerous Certificates of Need; partnering with congressional leaders and their staff on new legislation; dealing with corporate compliance issues; ensuring a strong and collaborative relationship with human resources; developing strategic partnerships in Illinois and around the world; negotiating an IT relationship to develop a unique software for the rehabilitation field; and working on patents, grants, and licensing arrangements as well as clinical trials to make dreams become innovations. At this moment, RIC is building a new state-of-the-art facility that will revolutionize the field of physical and rehabilitation medicine; it has been a fabulous experience to be involved with purchasing the land, participating in designing from the "inside out," and obtaining the appropriate state, regulatory, and community approvals as well as negotiating the myriad of contracts and overseeing the insurance for the project.

However, truly the best part of my job is the people with whom I spend each and every day. My small but very mighty team through the years has consisted of a core of lawyers, compliance officers and analysts, community affairs representatives, and ethics professionals as well as paralegals, board assistants, and administrative staff. The team shines and has accomplished great things while always being dedicated to RIC's mission and vision for the future. At RIC, we are committed to helping individuals to live to the best of their ability. I am also honored to be a member of an executive leadership team that is unmatched by any Fortune 500 company. They are a group of savvy individuals who act as innovators, advocates, and forward thinkers, but never forget the passion for our patients and their families.

To say that I have been fortunate is an understatement. A career that combines my interest in science with the skills of a litigator and the strategy of a corporate lawyer while never forgetting my first love of teaching is a rare but wonderful experience. I do not know what the future will bring, however, I know I will enjoy a life of learning and gratitude.

Continued

Suppliers and Vendors

Companies that provide medical, surgical, and pharmaceutical products and services to health care providers have specific legal needs relating to the health care industry as well. Suppliers and vendors are subject to complex regulations that govern the distribution of their products. To explore suppliers and vendors, search for trade associations for these organizations, many of which are based at the state and regional levels. Suppliers and vendors vary greatly in size and scope of business and may employ legal teams ranging from small to large.

Pharmaceutical and Medical Device Companies

Drug and medical device companies research, develop, and market medicines and technologies for health promotion and disease prevention. Their products range from nutritional items and pharmaceutical therapies to medical devices and laboratory diagnostics. Advances in drug and device technology, including the use of genomics and personalized medicine, continue to change this field rapidly. Drug and device companies employ attorneys to oversee all functions, including the highly regulated field of clinical research and clinical trials, manufacturing, and the marketing and sale of drugs and devices. These companies, more so than other health care employers, often look for attorneys with more specialized knowledge of intellectual property and patent law, as most drugs and devices are patented.

Insurers and Payors

Health insurance companies of all types hire lawyers to work on corporate, contractual, regulatory, reimbursement, and litigation matters. Health insurers face an ever-growing number of state and federal regulations, creating a need for experienced and knowledgeable attorneys and compliance officers. Many insurers and payors are based in and operate within specific geographic areas. For larger insurers, opportunities for health lawyers can be found on company websites.

Consulting Firms

Consulting firms assist academic medical centers, private medical practices, hospitals, ambulatory businesses, and other health care providers in improving their structure, efficiency, and financial bottom line. Health care consulting firms prefer to hire individuals with directly related, relevant health care experience as well as business experience. For more information about consulting work, see chapter 4.

Public Interest Law

Many public interest law organizations offer opportunities to represent underserved populations in areas relating to health law, including disability discrimination and benefits, Medicare and Medicaid coverage, government benefits and insurance, elder law, and others. Working in health law for a nonprofit entity can be as competitive as landing a law firm job. Many traditional public interest jobs related to health involve public benefits. The scope of health law is expanding. For example, medical-legal partnerships, in which attorneys partner with medical providers to assist patients with their legal needs, are increasingly common.

Public interest organizations differ from other "in-house" positions in that attorneys employed in public interest are most often involved in providing direct client services to individuals. In this way, public interest work is more like client representation at a law firm than a traditional in-house position. Some attorneys in public interest organizations also advise the organization on legal issues such as scope of services provided, tax-exempt status, and other matters.

Attorneys often cite salary as a concern in pursuing public interest work. In researching possible public interest jobs, it can be helpful to obtain the IRS 990 tax return forms for the nonprofit organization under consideration. Generally, a public interest organization will identify top salaries in its tax returns.[8] Newly minted attorneys going to work in public interest may earn between $30,000 and $70,000, depending on the organization's budget and location.

Public interest organizations are most often locally based, and the number of organizations varies widely based on geographic location. Searches can be conducted on a local level. For a comprehensive listing of many positions, the Public Service Jobs Directory (www.psjd.org, formerly PSLawNet) is an excellent resource. Many public interest organizations also participate in fellowship programs funded by outside agencies. Public interest fellowships, which often offer limited appointments within public interest organizations, are an excellent way to gain exposure to health care law in this area.

CAREER PROFILE

Amy Zimmerman
Director of the Chicago Medical-Legal Partnership for Children
Health and Disability Advocates

What if more doctors and lawyers worked together? Could people get healthier? Would their lives be better? The idea of working across disciplines to try to "cure" nonmedical factors that keep low-income, minority populations from thriving is at the cornerstone of the medical-legal partnership (MLP) approach.

One of the first MLPs in the country, the Chicago Medical-Legal Partnership for Children is a project of Health and Disability Advocates (HDA), a national health, education, and employment nonprofit. This innovative venture joins two powerful professions—law and medicine—to reduce health disparities among children.

The families that my team and I work with are typically minority, have medically complex children, and live below the poverty line. Some of them did not always live in poverty. Just having a child born with a disability can thrust a family into financial crisis. For our families, the hospital setting is often their second home. So we partner closely with renowned children's hospitals and specialty clinics in Chicago, including Lurie, La Rabida, and Comer, to train clinicians to spot and refer issues that can have a profound impact on child health. Our attorneys meet with families to troubleshoot. We use everything in our legal "toolbox"—administrative, judicial, and

---

8. These documents can be found by signing up for a free subscription to http://www .guidestar.org/ or http://nccs.urban.org/.

NOTES

legislative advocacy—to improve individual and overall access to quality health, developmental, educational, and income supports for children.

Over 20 years ago, when I graduated law school, there was no such thing as a medical-legal partnership. Now, there are hundreds of MLPs across the country, many of which we helped advise and grow. But in many ways, my career trajectory took me here. I began my career as a neighborhood legal services attorney at the Legal Assistance Foundation, eventually branching out to work in special projects, including HIV-AIDS, disability rights, and finally, children's rights. Next, I worked for the Chicago Lawyers' Committee for Civil Rights Under Law as the Associate Director in its Children's Health and Education Project. Finally, before assuming my current role directing the Chicago Medical-Legal Partnership for Children, I served as the Children's Policy Advisor to Illinois Attorney General Lisa Madigan.

What does it mean to direct the Chicago Medical-Legal Partnership for Children? My work is multifaceted, but there are core duties that support our unique service approach. I supervise a small but formidable staff of talented attorneys who provide trainings to providers and direct representation to our patient families, along with law students and attorney volunteers who assist in all facets of our work. Another important part of my job is to ensure that the medical teams at our partnership sites understand what we can do for them and their patients. Part of this involves organizing trainings for the medical residents. We recognize that if we are going to reshape the way medicine is practiced, we have to start by engaging doctors at the beginning of their careers. In addition, at our medical sites, I am engaged with quality assurance efforts and focused initiatives to constantly improve our communication, outreach, and impact.

Systemic advocacy initiatives comprise much of my day-to-day work, which is enormously gratifying. I have found that the best way to develop policy initiatives is to have them evolve from and be responsive to the real-life experiences of the families we represent. I have the opportunity to serve on a number of statewide advisory groups, and I am an appointed member of the Illinois Interagency Council on Early Intervention, the Governor's Lead Safe Housing Advisory Council, and the Attorney General's Special Education Advisory Committee. The ability to view programs and services through the lens of serving children with special health care needs allows me to provide informed recommendations and analyses of federal and state programs to relevant decision makers. This special vantage point also allows me to identify and work with stakeholders to successfully move forward legislative proposals in the Illinois General Assembly. One of the laws we worked on requires that school districts implement children's special education services within ten school attendance days.

Continued

My team and I have the privilege of working with enlightened, compassionate, and committed doctors and medical team members, who understand that medicine alone can't always heal a family in crisis. It is empowering and rewarding to see how much our "physician champions" recognize and appreciate what law brings to the table. Doctors we work with have told us that before our medical–legal partnership began, they avoided asking questions that could generate legal referrals, because they had nowhere to send families. Consequently, legal problems felt insurmountable, and health concerns often became secondary concerns for families. Now, those families are empowered.

On average, vulnerable families have five unmet legal needs. The doctors we work with take the time (of which they have no excess) to identify these needs and refer families to us for legal care. But their participation doesn't end there; in fact, that is just the beginning of their engagement. They write letters to secure necessary benefits, testify at hearings, advocate for policy and legislative initiatives, and work with us to develop trainings, formulate research ideas, and help secure grants and funding to power the work.

None of this is lost on the families that we serve. By joining medical care, social support services, and legal assistance in an accessible, well-coordinated, comprehensive, and family-centered care setting, we help build a "medical home" for some of Chicago's most vulnerable children and work preventively to tackle many issues before a crisis occurs.

Most of this important work is supported by grants and donations. Truly, the only downside to working in a public interest practice setting is funding insecurity. Thankfully, the rewards are well worth the gamble.

Health Care Trade Organizations

Health care trade associations represent, and serve as advocates and leaders for, their respective member organizations. There are national, state, and local organizations. Trade associations and professional organizations require a broad range of legal counsel and services, including regulatory, tort reform, and contract issues in the legislative, executive, and administrative arenas.

Attorneys who work for trade organizations often perform duties similar to those of lawyers who work in-house at other types of companies. These organizations represent one type of provider or supplier or one part of the industry and are focused on one particular perspective on issues. Attorneys for trade organizations are responsible for all legal matters encountered by the organization and oversee the organization's policy and advocacy efforts and legal advice dispensed to members. Trade organizations work in legislation, advocacy, lobbying, publishing of scholarly materials, and more. Because of the diverse work that trade organizations do, their attorneys can expect to work on many different areas of law. Trade organization attorneys perform tasks such as crafting policy positions, lobbying, writing amicus briefs, advising the organization on legislative and regulatory issues, and explaining the law to the organization's leadership and constituents.

Attorneys working for trade organizations tend to earn less than those at firms. However, there is a large variation in the amount of pay and work depending on the size and nature of the organization. Please see Appendix C for a list of national trade associations.

Chapter 4

Nontraditional Jobs in Health Law

Not all law school graduates practice law. Many choose never to practice law, while others practice for many years before transitioning to a "nontraditional" career where legal knowledge or the analytical, verbal, writing, research, and advocacy skills learned in law school are particularly transferable and advantageous. Chapter 3 examines a variety of traditional health law practice settings. Alternatively, this chapter provides an overview of several nontraditional health care–based career options well suited for attorneys' transferable skill sets, including consulting, academia, public health, and nonprofit work. This chapter is not meant to be a comprehensive listing of all alternative career options, but rather, a brief introduction to common avenues worth exploration.

Compliance

Compliance programs are designed to assist the organization in complying with the law. It is not surprising that lawyers have gravitated toward the role and that the health care industry has looked favorably on legal training as a pathway to the compliance officer profession.

Compliance programs are not unique to the health care industry, but since the mid-1990s compliance programs have become increasingly common among health care organizations, if not voluntarily then as a condition for continuing to participate in the Medicare program upon settling regulatory noncompliance issues with the U.S. Department of Health and Human

Services. There is now a move to make compliance programs mandatory. The Patient Protection and Affordable Care Act of 2010 (PPACA) mandated that skilled nursing facilities and Medicare Advantage plans adopt compliance programs as well as requiring any new provider or supplier enrolling in Medicare in 2014 to adopt a compliance program. While compliance programs were once seen as the province of highly risk-averse organizations or a type of penalty for noncompliance, they are now being seen increasingly as essential corporate preventive measures in an intense regulatory environment. The complexity and pervasiveness of the health care regulatory landscape has made the compliance officer role ideally suited for lawyers.

Before discussing what a compliance officer does and how lawyers work within the role, it is important to describe what a compliance program is. The basis of a health care organization's compliance program structure, as well as the PPACA's mandate, comes from the Federal Sentencing Guidelines' (FSG) willingness to lessen a criminally convicted corporation's culpability score if it had an "effective" compliance program in place. Chapter 8 of the FSG sets out several elements that must be in place in a compliance program in order for it to be considered effective. The various elements essentially describe a compliance program as an organized initiative to educate on, audit, and respond to specific legal risk areas. The FSG is neutral on what subject-matter areas the compliance program should cover, though the program should presumably cover the area of conduct that the conviction covered. The various elements of an effective compliance program as described in the FSG were picked up in the PPACA's mandatory compliance programs.

In the development of health care compliance programs, a significant series of Health and Human Services-Office of Inspector General (HHS-OIG) documents were published between the time the FSG first exhorted organizations to adopt compliance programs and the PPACA's adoption of a mandatory model. The HHS-OIG released numerous "compliance program guidances" (OIG CPGs) between 1998 and 2008 that described compliance programs for specific sectors of the health care industry. Although the OIG CPGs sketched outlines for "voluntary" compliance program adoption, by the late 1990s it became commonplace for most health care organizations that did not have a compliance program to be required to adopt one by OIG as a condition for settling significant, and sometimes insignificant, matters of noncompliance that in some way touched on reimbursement from federal health care programs. These agreements are known as Corporate Integrity Agreements, and the organization's commitments to implement and maintain the core elements of a compliance program in accordance with the applicable OIG CPG are codified here. Although compliance programs remained technically voluntary until the PPACA's passage, it was highly prudent for health care organizations to adopt a compliance program, or be subject to a federally designed program that would be much more difficult and costly to manage than a compliance program of the organization's own design.

Over time, the foundational documents for the structure of a compliance program, and consequently, the duties of a compliance officer, have been a mixture of the FSG's elements, the OIG CPGs' recommendations, and the stringent terms of Corporate Integrity Agreements. The PPACA is now added to the mix in defining the compliance officer's role.

The health care industry is one of the most highly regulated sectors of the U.S. economy. This book aptly demonstrates this assertion. The most common areas covered by health care compliance programs include (1) federal health care program reimbursement; (2) relationships with referral sources; (3) privacy and security of health information; (4) engagement in biomedical research; and (5) tax-exemption status. Health care organizations have a mix of these subject matters and others, depending upon each organization's unique risks and the lines of business it undertakes. But the common feature of all these areas is that they represent bodies of laws and contain a labyrinth of regulations. The number of agencies interested in these subject-matter areas is not typically confined to one, and so not only parsing the rules but responding to enforcement is a cross-agency challenge.

None of the documents referenced in this section defines the education or training that a compliance officer should have. This allows organizations to design the compliance officer position in any way it chooses. None of the government oversight agencies has said that it expects the role of the compliance officer to be filled by a lawyer. No complete data exist on the number of compliance officer positions that are filled by lawyers, but there is little doubt that the percentage is significant. A health care compliance officer role is situated well for a lawyer because of the high complexity of regulatory obligations a compliance program must educate on, audit, and respond to.

The posture of legal rules that health care organizations must comply with presents challenges for individuals who do not have legal training or do not have regular access to legal counsel. Another forum may explore the justice of these types of laws that are virtually unreadable by laypeople, but the reality is that they must be dealt with. Noncompliance has significant consequences and possibly catastrophic fines and penalties.

When a compliance officer is also a lawyer, the question of reporting becomes important: is the organization looking to the compliance officer for legal advice? Most lawyers who serve in the capacity of compliance officer and do not report to the general counsel disclaim providing legal advice and fill the position in an administrative capacity. This is also often the case even when a compliance officer reports to the general counsel and the compliance officer is a lawyer. Since it is not necessary that the compliance officer be a lawyer, it is difficult to argue that a lawyer in the compliance officer's job is providing legal advice unless the advice is specifically characterized and framed as legal advice.

Although lawyers serving as compliance officers typically do not provide legal advice to the organization, their legal training is valuable in interpreting the complex regulatory law impacting the organization. A lawyer also brings training and experience in assessing risk priorities and managing legal exposure. Clearly, the knowledge and skills a lawyer receives from his or her legal education fit nicely with the role a compliance officer serves in assisting an organization's compliance with the law.

CAREER PROFILE

John E. Steiner Jr.
Chief Compliance and Privacy Officer
and Associate General Counsel
Cancer Treatment Centers of America

Over the past 30 years, I have worked in a large law firm (Katten Muchin Rosenman), the nation's premier hospital trade association (American Hospital Association [AHA]), an international referral center with specialization in heart diseases (Cleveland Clinic Health System), a state university, a flagship medical center (University of Kentucky Healthcare), and a national hospital system specializing in advanced, complex cancer treatment (Cancer Treatment Centers of America). In those roles, I have been fortunate to be able to combine rigorous legal practice for a diverse health care client base with national policy and advocacy work in Washington, D.C., on behalf of America's hospitals and health systems. One element of my work involved serving as the principal drafter, on behalf of the AHA, of the Model Voluntary Compliance Program Guidance for Hospitals, which was published by the Office of Inspector General of the Department of Health and Human Services. After serving with the AHA, I was recruited to be the first Chief Compliance Officer in the history of the Cleveland Clinic Health System. In that role, my primary duty was to design, implement, and oversee the administration of a voluntary, enterprise-wide corporate compliance program. Those three tasks—design, implement, and administer—are fundamental to the work of a chief compliance officer. Thus, my roles after the Cleveland Clinic call for similar skill sets.

Those skills include active listening to "internal clients"—that is, personnel working in patient accounts, finance, information technology, health information management, pharmacy, and medical staff office, and leaders in clinical affairs, senior management, and governance positions. The methods and techniques for building and sustaining an effective corporate compliance program also require these skills: solid leadership traits, excellent communication skills, experienced judgment when assessing compliance situations, and—in my opinion—the ability to "think like a lawyer." I mention this because not all compliance professionals are lawyers, though many are, especially those individuals with "Chief" titles and frequent access to members of the board of directors.

My substantive knowledge and skills are broad, the result of having worked extensively in both the not-for-profit/tax-exempt as well as the proprietary health care delivery arenas. I mention this point here as an example of the possible breadth of issues that "touch" compliance (either directly or indirectly). That said, a compliance professional ideally should have a collaborative working relationship with inside counsel, internal audit, and other support areas (especially finance). Because many positions in large, complex health care systems work through matrixed reporting relationships, clarity of communication and collegiality are critical success factors for a chief compliance officer.

An important element of my work, as Chief Compliance Officer and Privacy Officer, is to think, plan, and execute proactively. To do so, I generally assemble working teams or ad hoc groups for specific projects. For example, when the HITECH amendments to HIPAA (Health Insurance

Continued

Portability and Accountability Act) were passed, a small group under my leadership analyzed and drafted memos and tools that we put into operation across the enterprise to comply with HITECH. Also, our department prepares quarterly, written reports for the Executive Compliance Committee that address core (or "mission critical") risk areas. Those areas include hospital-specific issues, generally related to sustaining a compliant revenue cycle; physician documentation and coding compliance; HIPAA Privacy Rule and Security Rule compliance; clinical research compliance; pharmacy compliance (especially for cancer pharmacological agents); and many other sub-issues within the these categories.

In my role at each of the last three health care organizations, I have reported directly to the chief executive officer and the board of directors. I oversee a relatively small staff of direct reports and indirectly supervise many others. Those individuals have diverse educational backgrounds and working experiences, yet all work well together as a cohesive group. One of my personnel management tasks involves gauging how to assign work over the course of a quarter or six months, as priorities change. Those changes may be internal (e.g., business plans) or external (e.g., changes to federal or state law).

I mentioned the importance of being proactive. I enjoyed the opportunity to be an advocate for AHA and actually effect changes in the law. For example, I worked extensively with CMS (Centers for Medicare and Medicaid Services) to introduce more procedural due process protections in the enforcement of the Emergency Medical Treatment and Labor Act (EMTALA). I also wrote nearly all of the AHA's regulatory comments and congressional testimony over the years on the Anti-Kickback Statute and the Stark law (Ethics in Patient Referrals Act). That work allowed me to interact and match wits directly with the top lawyers and policy advisors at CMS, the Office of Inspector General, and other federal executive agencies—all with the purpose of making it easier for our hospitals to deliver patient care and receive inherently reasonable reimbursement for their services.

Likewise, when I assumed the Chief Compliance Officer roles at the above-named health systems, I thoroughly enjoyed being received as a seasoned advisor versus an "enforcement type." That is a skill that takes time to develop and requires keen appreciation of the daily demands and pressures placed on clinical and support personnel as well as fellow executives. I also enjoy mentoring my staff and others within the health system when I explain how our program is designed, implemented, and administered. That insight is critical to the success of an effective compliance program. In short, it is rewarding when people (whom you may or may not supervise) grasp the basic legal premise that we are accountable for what we know or should have known as participants in health care delivery. If your compliance program can hit that mark—you're on your way.

Consulting

Consultants serve an important role for all types of evolving organizations, but in the ever-changing health care field, they are even more essential. A consultant or consulting firm is often hired by health care organizations that are implementing new business, legal, human capital, financing, or compliance strategies. This job is not unique to health care as consultants serve in almost every industry. However, consultants often work in industries that are complex and highly regulated, such as health care. Organizations often cannot resolve all complex issues internally, requiring them to seek the outside knowledge and experience of a consultant or consulting firm.

Health care consulting groups often hire lawyers as consultants because of their understanding of the law and their well-honed research, analysis, and writing skills. Health care consultants will often work closely with outside legal counsel to provide health care clients with legal or business strategy recommendations. Legal counsel generally provide legal advice and draft documents such as acquisition agreements, whereas consultants deliver other types of work product that do not necessarily require a law license to draft. Projects that a consultant may encounter when working with a health care client include implementing clinical integration strategies, such as the creation of accountable care organizations or the implementation of value-based purchasing, bundled payment, or quality initiatives; evaluating and structuring mergers and acquisitions or strategic business line restructuring; and evaluating or creating regulatory compliance and risk management strategies and solutions.

Other defining characteristics differentiate consulting work from more traditional legal career paths. Historically, because the majority of a consultant's work was done at the client's office, consulting was associated with frequent travel. Although many consulting jobs still require some degree of travel, technology has lessened the demand in some cases. Additionally, consultants do not all work on a billable hour system and are at times paid by project instead of by time increments, which is still less common than in law firms.

Positions in consulting are a great fit for attorneys interested in or with a background in business, finance, health care administration, or management. Because consulting work often combines legal and business strategy, it can be a good fit for lawyers looking for opportunities to become more involved in the business community and work with other nonlegal professionals. Many attorneys working in consulting feel that the problem solving, research, and writing skills honed in law school provide great preparation for the strategic thinking and analysis required in consulting.

CAREER PROFILE

Kyle Vasquez
Vice President
Murer Consultants Inc.

I am in what some call an alternative health law career as I am currently a Vice President at Murer Consultants Inc., a midsize health care consulting firm. Murer Consultants Inc. provides unique and highly specialized assistance to health systems looking to enhance their bottom line while maintaining compliance with applicable federal and state regulations. Regulatory-focused health care consultants are becoming increasingly more common due to health systems' interest in working with experts who understand not only relevant regulations but also the business and operational issues that may be involved. Many health system providers are looking for innovative solutions in the ever-changing health care environment. As a result, a number of boutique health care firms, consulting and legal, are stepping outside the box to provide a different type of health care solution using unique fee structures. I am pleased to be part of that movement at Murer.

I received my law degree from the John Marshall Law School in Chicago and a BA in economics from the University of Illinois. During my time in school, I was constantly reminded that my goal was to find a career that involved health care, and I was still unsure how to meet this goal. I did not see myself as a traditional courtroom attorney. With the help of some key mentors, I discovered the health law program at the Loyola University Chicago School of Law. Following law school, I obtained my Master of Laws (LLM) degree in Health Law from Loyola, and it was one of the best decisions I have ever made. There are a number of similar programs across the country, but I really felt at home at Loyola because its LLM program focused on the legal and regulatory aspects of health care transactions and compliance—in other words, the business and operations of health care.

The LLM program opened up a number of opportunities for me, including some in-house internships at various health care organizations. These internships exposed me to issues commonly faced by health systems as well as to the methodology that health systems employ to make day-to-day legal, business, and strategic decisions. When I reached the end of the LLM program, the consulting opportunity at Murer Consultants Inc. presented itself. At first, I was somewhat reluctant to take the position because it was not a traditional law firm job. In law school, I felt that there was a big push to get students into law firms and that there was very little focus on alternative careers. However, after speaking with colleagues and mentors and considering my skill set and interest in an alternative setting, I took a chance and joined Murer Consultants Inc. This turned out to be a very wise choice and has worked out very well.

As a Vice President at Murer, I manage a wide range of health care consulting projects on a national scale, and I have also taken on a business development role. My practice has developed and evolved over time, which is common in the health care community, particularly in consulting. As a result, I have gained a wealth of great experience, including working directly with large health system clients on a number of different initiatives. I have focused a great deal of my career on the federal 340B Drug Pricing Program (340B) and related regulations. The 340B program is designed to provide certain safety-net providers with significant discounts on pharmaceuticals that they provide to their patients. In short, the 340B program is a mechanism that safety-net providers can use to enhance the care that they provide to their needy populations. The 340B program is a highly regulated area with a significant self-regulation component, which is why I believe my legal training, specifically my LLM, is invaluable. I took a particular interest in the 340B program early in my career and made a point of devoting a significant amount of my time, both at work and at home, to developing my 340B knowledge and client base.

I work with health systems and health centers to maximize their 340B savings while remaining compliant with federal and state regulations. In my 340B practice, I also conduct comprehensive 340B feasibility assessments and assist with implementation of unique strategies to access 340B drug savings, such as the conversion of physician practices to hospital

Continued

provider–based departments and the development of contract pharmacy networks with local retailers, such as Walgreen's and CVS.

In addition to implementing strategic 340B initiatives, I use my experience and expertise to provide clients with on-site assistance with Office of Pharmacy Affairs and other governmental 340B program audits. I also conduct external compliance reviews of 340B programs and contract pharmacy networks to prepare 340B providers for potential government audits.

At Murer, I am actively involved in developing innovative physician alignment strategies, such as clinical comanagement and accountable care models. My practice also focuses on regulatory review, compliance, and development activities for new health care facilities, including general acute care hospitals, multicampus hospitals, psychiatric facilities, exempted rehabilitation providers, federally qualified health centers (FQHCs), and other key players in the health care continuum. Additionally, I have expertise in the areas of electronic health records incentives (HITECH), disproportionate share hospital (DSH) designations, and federal and state grant funding.

At Murer, I use my ability to research and analyze federal and state regulations to find programs that positively contribute to health providers' bottom lines. We typically meet with high-level staff at health care systems who provide us with a set of facts, and we identify potential cost savings or revenue-generating measures that fit within the systems' existing framework. Our ability to quickly spot issues and opportunities, and subsequently present viable solutions, has led to many successful relationships and projects that continue to grow.

What gives me great enjoyment at Murer is knowing that there are endless opportunities out there, and I have the flexibility and the support to pursue new projects or new topics if I feel they are both viable and valuable to our firm. I have a number of colleagues outside Murer who feel they are working on the same topic or document day in and day out. I know that is never going to be an issue in my current position. Because of this flexibility, I gained some really valuable experience at an early age, including consistent direct contact with executives at our health system clients. As I continue to develop and serve in a senior position, I manage projects, teams, and all aspects of client relationships. This has helped me expand on ongoing projects as well as develop new projects and clients. I believe this is a valuable skill set whether you are working in a traditional law firm environment or an alternative environment. I credit Murer as well as a number of key mentors who have provided some very valuable advice throughout my career, including mentors from Loyola's health law program.

Business

Because health care is so highly regulated, a background in health law can position someone very well for a career in business. Typically an attorney will gain legal experience for a few years before moving into a managerial or executive position. However, this is not always the case. Whether because of a desire to mix an interest in business with health law or because an opportunity presents itself, health care attorneys are increasingly moving into business-oriented positions.

Further, as technology becomes an ever-larger driver of health care innovation, many attorneys find themselves drawn to high-tech businesses where they are expected to bring their legal knowledge to bear while working in a managerial (or sometimes blended legal and managerial) capacity.

A career in the business side of the health care industry can be tremendously rewarding. That said, care should be taken to ensure that this career step has been adequately thought through. It will likely be very difficult to step back onto the "attorney track" if you have been away from legal services for any significant length of time. Accordingly, individuals considering a business career as an option should carefully think through their reasons for pursuing this career choice and make sure that their talents and desires that first drove them to attend law school will be fulfilled in the opportunity under consideration.

Academia

Careers in advanced education for health lawyers are available in a variety of institutional settings, including law, medical, and public health schools. Traditional tenure-track, clinical, and non-tenure-track (adjunct) teaching positions are available. There are also administrative positions. Additionally, many practicing attorneys serve as adjunct faculty members at educational institutions. The following are just a few examples of educational settings in which a health law background can be beneficial.

Legal Education

With health law projected to be one of the fastest growing areas of legal employment, legal education in this area is expanding. Although the health law field is relatively new compared to some areas of practice, a number of law schools now offer health law concentration curriculums. With the ever-increasing complexity of health law and the expansion of health law concentrations, law schools will continue to need faculty trained in health law to educate the next generation of health lawyers and to develop and structure health law programs.

Tenure-Track Faculty Positions

For many years, tenure-track faculty positions were the staple of legal education. Professors who attain tenure are given lifetime employment and can only be terminated for very serious reasons or extreme institutional financial hardship. In addition to job security, tenure provides a great deal of freedom for the recipient to pursue scholarly research and publication. Over the course of at least several years, a tenure-track faculty member's progress in teaching, writing, and service is monitored. At the end of this probationary period, the law faculty vote on whether to grant tenure to the professor.

Professors in tenure-track positions develop course materials for their respective subject areas and are expected to commit a substantial amount of time to scholarly research and publication. Tenure-track positions often require professors to teach a portion of the first-year curriculum but may also include teaching advanced specialty classes in health law. Those pursuing tenure-track positions should expect to balance classroom teaching with scholarly publication, with the exact balance depending on the institution.

Securing a tenure-track position is a highly competitive process about which several excellent guides exist, including *Becoming a Law Professor: A Candidate's Guide*, published by the ABA.[1] It is important to address the reality that tenure-track law professor positions are very difficult to

---

1. BRANNON P. DENNING, MARCIA L. MCCORMICK & JEFFREY M. LIPSHAW, BECOMING A LAW PROFESSOR (American Bar Association 2010).

obtain; the majority of law school faculty members graduated from elite law schools. In fact, nearly 70 percent of all law school faculty members graduated from ten law schools.[2] In addition to graduating from a top-tier law school, if one wants to pursue a tenure-track position, scholarly publication as well as membership in an esteemed law journal during law school are often prerequisites. Many hiring committees also highly value judicial clerkship experience, particularly on the federal level.

Excellent research, writing, and teaching skills are critical for tenure-track teaching. Serving on a law school faculty is extremely rewarding, and many professors enjoy the one-on-one interactions with their students and involve students in their research and writing projects. Professors spend a great deal of time researching and writing scholarly articles. A good track record of research and publication is often the most critical criterion for achieving tenure status. Attorneys interested in pursuing these traditional law faculty spots should aim to write several scholarly articles before applying for positions.

Non-tenure-track faculty positions also exist in legal education. Non-tenure-track positions often have many of the same job requirements as tenure-track positions but offer a lesser degree of job security. Clinical teaching positions, discussed in the next section, are nontenured positions or have their own "tenure" requirements. Legal writing and adjunct positions are also generally nontenured positions.

Clinical Teaching

Over the last ten years, legal education has increasingly emphasized the value of clinical legal experience for skills training and as a supplement to classroom learning. This shift has led to the creation of a variety of legal clinics at law schools across the country. At the helm of these clinics are clinical professors who often did not follow the traditional tenure track. Clinical professors are more likely to have practiced law before moving to

---

2. *See, e.g.,* Lawrence B. Solum, *Entry Level Hiring Survey 2010,* LEGAL THEORY BLOG (Apr. 12, 2010), http://lsolum.typepad.com/legaltheory/2010/04/entry-level-hiring-survey-2010 .html.

academia. Most law schools allow clinical faculty members to attain tenure or secure a type of longer term contractual commitment from the school.[3]

Clinical professors are generally drawn to the work for two main reasons: to provide representation to low-income clients facing legal issues and to provide real-world legal experience to participating students. Typically, clinical education faculty members are able to focus primarily on the teaching and mentorship aspects of the job, unlike tenure-track faculty members who must also focus on research. Law schools with health law–related clinical programs would be an ideal intersection of interests for the legal professional who wants to teach while continuing to practice health law. Popular areas of health law clinical work include cases involving Social Security and disability law, access to health services, medical-legal partnerships (in which clinics partner directly with health care providers to address legal issues impacting health), and clinics focusing on the legal effects of certain health issues, including HIV/AIDS, mental health, cancer, and more.

Clinical teaching positions are a good fit for attorneys interested in academia but also wanting to continue practicing law. Important skills include teaching, both in substantive legal areas and professional skills; mentoring; and project management. Clinical professors are often responsible for all operations of their clinics, including case management, teaching and training materials, and budgeting and office administration.

Adjunct Faculty

Adjunct faculty positions are the most common opportunities for health lawyers in legal academia. Law schools commonly hire adjunct faculty members who have expertise in a particular field to teach one or two courses in a specialty practice area. An adjunct teaching position capitalizes on the specialized knowledge of the health law practitioner who is typically advanced in his or her career. Taking classes taught by adjunct faculty can benefit law students who learn from practicing attorneys who have a wealth of practical experience. Adjunct professors' practical experience can translate into a more skills-based educational environment for students, as opposed to

---

3. *Id.*

the traditional doctrinal courses. Individuals interested in adjunct teaching are advised to communicate their desire to the academic dean or health law program director at their area law school(s).

Medical Schools

Medicine is one of the most highly regulated industries, and for that reason health care workers are continually faced with issues that have legal significance. Consequently, medical schools across the country have added a legal component to their curriculum, often incorporated into bioethics course work. Medical schools employ medical law professors to educate aspiring health care providers about the intersection of law and medicine. Similar to legal academia, medical education incorporates full-time and adjunct faculty members. The unique institutional setting helps shape the health care educator's role. Health lawyers working at medical schools can generally expect to work alongside medical educators to help illustrate the intersection between the law and medicine, especially as it relates to bioethics and patient safety. Additionally, these professors may expect to serve as the liaison for the legal profession to medical students who may be exposed for the first time to health care legal issues during this formative time in their professional careers.

Other Programs

Health law professionals are not limited to solely pursuing careers at law or medical schools. Academic programs such as business schools, public health schools, and nursing and allied health schools, among others, hire health law professionals as educators. Because health law and policy impact the entire industry, all kinds of professionals can benefit from having a better understanding of this area.

Higher Education Administration

Attorneys also work in areas of academic administration in law, medicine, and other settings. Many staff positions within law schools are filled by attorneys. With an ever-growing number of specialty health law programs, more schools are seeking to hire administrators experienced in the legal field and with a knowledge of health law to help develop a specialized curriculum and student activities and programming. Even aside from special-ized positions within health law programs, many law school staff members serve as student affairs and career counselors, run externship programs, or work in admissions. These positions require excellent problem solving and management skills, as most administrators deal with a variety of student issues, event planning, database management, and budget management. Many attorneys seeking a law-related job outside traditional legal practice find working in a law school setting to be very rewarding. Similar positions working with students and services are available in other graduate school settings, including medical and nursing schools and schools of public health.

Other Areas

A law degree can be an excellent background for careers in public health, nonprofit organizations, and research. Each area offers unique personal and professional benefits.

Public Health

Public health professionals focus their efforts on the health of a specific population or on a specific disease. Public health law differs from other types of health law in that "health care law primarily deals with regulating medical practice and personal health care, and mandating and regulating the health care delivery system, its financing, and conducting research. Public health law, on the other hand, is primarily concerned with the government's powers and duties to assure conditions under which populations will be as healthy as possible."[4] Examples of public health initiatives include manda-tory seatbelt laws, pollution controls, and food and drug regulations.

Public health professionals often research, draft, or advocate on behalf of public health policy, regulations, and legislation at the municipal, state, or federal government level. Positions are found at all levels of government.

---

4. Barbara A. DeBuono et al., Advancing Healthy Populations: The Pfizer Guide to Careers in Public Health (2003), *available at* http://www.soph.uab.edu/isoph/pfizer/PHCareerGuide.pdf.

The Department of Health and Human Services (HHS) and the National Institutes of Health (NIH) are prominent national institutions to consider for careers. For those interested in global health, international organizations and government positions should be explored. Most state and local governments have a number of public health initiatives and hire professionals to address specific public health issues faced by populations within those areas.

In addition to holding government positions, lawyers commonly work for public interest and nonprofit organizations focusing on public health. These opportunities include advocating or lobbying for a particular issue or area of public health—for example, immigration or lead poisoning prevention. This can be a very rewarding career path.

A legal background can be very beneficial to this line of work, although some specialization in health is likely required. Law students interested in public health should consider taking classes in health law, public health, administrative law, constitutional law, food and drug law, environmental law, and legislative process. Students should also consider an externship, internship, or clerkship at a public health organization or governmental entity. Lawyers looking to transition to public health may consider pursuing a Master of Public Health (MPH) or a Master of Laws (LLM) degree, which are discussed in Chapter 5.

Nonprofit Organizations

The United States has an estimated 2.3 million nonprofit organizations in operation.[5] While the overall number of employees in the U.S. economy has been declining since 2008, nonprofit sector employment has increased in terms of both numbers and wages; between 2000 and 2010, nonprofit sector employment increased 17 percent (wages increased 29 percent) while business sector employment decreased 6 percent (wages decreased 1 percent).[6] As a result, nonprofits offer plenty of nontraditional career opportunities for the trained attorney seeking mission-driven employment.

---

5. NAT'L CTR FOR CHARITABLE STATISTICS, *The Nonprofit Almanac 2012*, http://nccsdataweb.urban.org/NCCS/extracts/nonprofitalmanacflyerpdf.pdf (last visited Mar. 24, 2014).

6. *Id.*

Generally, the nonprofit health care sector seeks to improve or meet the health care needs of our growing population. Such a complex and immense mission has resulted in a combination of many different types of nonprofit health care entities: hospitals, nursing facilities, higher education organizations, trade or professional organizations, public health programs, and other medical and community health programs, among others. Many attorneys will find that the skills they learned in law school or while practicing law will easily translate to a career in the nonprofit health care world. Nonprofit organizations operating with fewer resources and leaner staffs may be quicker to hire an employee with knowledge of law and policy. Specifically transferable skills include research and writing, communication and public speaking skills, advocacy skills, problem-solving skills, and understanding of public policy, the law, and strategic planning. Nonprofit positions appropriate for a trained health care attorney may include, among others, policy analyst, researcher, project manager, grant writer, director of grant and government relations, administrator, or executive director. Additionally, nonprofit organizations offer great opportunities for attorneys interested in policy work. These organizations often focus on policy and advocacy and are seen as community leaders in the locations in which they work. Therefore, they offer tremendous opportunity to influence national, state, and local law and policy.

A nonprofit health care organization will be a particularly good fit if you are dedicated to the organization's mission. Keep in mind that because nonprofits operate with tighter margins and smaller staffs, you will likely be expected to contribute outside your specific department or job title. Other considerations include the following:

- *Additional Education:* Those interested in pursuing a nontraditional legal job with a nonprofit organization should consider taking any law courses focusing on business finance, business management, and nonprofit law or policy. In addition, a business (MBA), health care (MHA or MPH), or public policy degree (MPP) would prepare you well for a nonprofit position.
- *Financial Considerations:* Because nonprofit salaries are typically lower than private sector salaries, paying off your law school investment may

take longer than expected or desired. However, there are loan forgiveness programs that should be explored. Additionally, because small nonprofits may not be able to financially contribute to your continued training and development (CLE education seminars, etc.), you may be responsible for those costs.

- *Finding the Job:* Nonprofit jobs may be harder to find because nonprofit organizations often do not have the financial ability to hire recruiters or widely distribute open position postings. Familiarizing yourself with these positions requires a great deal of local networking and research in the communities in which they operate.

Chapter 5

Before You Apply: Essential Preliminary Steps for Health Law Job Seekers

This chapter is designed to help law students, lawyers transitioning to health law, and lawyers changing paths within health law begin their job search. Before you are ready to apply for jobs, there are steps you should take to make yourself an attractive candidate. This chapter will begin by addressing the essential preliminary steps for your job search, including gaining knowledge, monitoring the market, and developing your network. Next, specific information for law students interested in pursuing a career in health law is presented. Finally, strategic advice for lawyers transitioning to or changing paths within health law is provided.

Gaining Knowledge and Monitoring the Market

While there are many steps to securing a position in health law, the starting point is assuring that you can present yourself as a credible candidate. Doing so requires that you master a core body of industry (business), legal, and policy knowledge. Specific avenues to achieve this, and then to begin your search, are discussed next.

Obtaining Knowledge and Skills Specific to Health Law

When exploring a potential career in health law, it is essential to begin developing knowledge and skills in the field. Regardless of where you are in your legal career, mastering some basic competencies in health law will demonstrate your interest and prepare you for practice in the area. There are many ways to do this. National, state, and local bar associations offer events related to health law, ranging from basic primers to specialty topics. Many bar associations sponsor sections in health law, and there are also national and state bar associations dedicated solely to health law. Universities often hold symposia and conferences on different aspects of health care, particularly in law schools, schools of public health, and medical and nursing schools. Trade associations and health-related professional organizations also provide trainings and seminars on health law topics. Opportunities can range from simple webinars to multiday, in-person sessions. These educational opportunities are an excellent way for someone at any skill level to begin exploring topics in the health law field.

Depending on the stage of your career, there are other educational opportunities in the field. These include pursuing specialized law school course work and extracurricular activities as well as advanced degrees and certifications (which are discussed in more detail later in this chapter). The sections to follow detail the opportunities available to law school students and attorneys to increase knowledge and skills specific to health law.

Although it is designed for law students, the skills chart later in this chapter is an excellent tool for anyone considering a career in health law. Because the field of health law is vast and complex, there are many topics and skills to explore. This chart identifies some basic and specialty skill areas within health law. Students and attorneys alike can seek out opportunities to become familiar with the topics listed in order to develop a basic knowledge of the field. These competencies are critical to demonstrating that one has the skills necessary to work in the field of health law.

Monitoring the Health Law Market

When pursuing new career opportunities, it is very important to monitor the specific area in which you are seeking employment. Monitoring the market is advantageous for several reasons. First, it is important to know which areas of health law are hiring and in which practice settings. You can track this information generally by monitoring the news and reading the newspaper. By joining a professional organization, you will have access to newsletters, publications, podcasts, and job postings. The American Bar Association's Health Law Section provides a wealth of information that can aid you in your job search. Many health law firms also publish newsletters and other publications about changes in legislation, regulations, or important court decisions that can signal the need for hiring in specific areas.

In addition to providing insight into hiring trends, monitoring the health law market is important for job interviews. Having an understanding of new developments in health law can be very important to demonstrating your interest and expertise in the field during interviews and while networking. Very good resources that can help you stay aware of recent developments include national newspapers such as the *New York Times* and the *Wall Street Journal*, Bloomberg BNA (formerly the Bureau of National Affairs [BNA]) publications, journals such as *Modern Healthcare*, and publications/ newsletters/e-newsletters from local, state, and national bar associations.

Developing Your Network

While you should absolutely apply for health law positions that are posted on websites and through professional associations and the like, most successful searches for positions in the health law field result from networking. This section lays out the basics of networking.

The Importance of Networking

Networking is simply meeting people, gathering information, and developing a relationship with individuals who can assist you. As you begin your job search, it will be very beneficial to meet lawyers who can give you advice, perspective, mentoring, introductions to other connections in the field, and sometimes job leads. Networking is not so much about who you currently know—although that helps—it is about who you meet and with whom you develop a relationship. All facets of your life can be enhanced by developing a strong network—including your personal and professional lives.

Networking can take place anywhere—in an elevator, on an airplane, at a bar association meeting—anywhere two people are talking and building a relationship. The topic of the conversation is not as important as building rapport and establishing a level of trust and credibility.

To some people who do not understand how to network, networking can have a bad connotation. Some incorrectly believe that networking involves "schmoozing" and "working a room." Asking for a job is not networking. Never, ever ask for a job when you are networking. It is the fastest way to end a conversation, because most people you meet will not have a job to give you. What they will have are their expertise, time, ideas, and information, which may lead to a relationship and to the possibility of a job sometime in the future. Meeting with a practicing attorney to gather information about that person's career path and practice area is networking, and you should begin to hone this skill during your law school career and beyond.

Why Networking Works

Distinguishing yourself from other applicants is essential to obtaining an interview. It is not unusual for a law firm to place a job announcement on an Internet job site and within days have hundreds of résumés from a single posting. Career counseling professionals estimate that almost 70 percent of all jobs that are filled are never advertised[1]—no newspaper or Internet ad, no placement on a company website, no professional recruiter or headhunter, no career fair. So how do people learn about these opportunities? Current employees of the company often tell their connections when a position is opening and may help them receive interviews. All this occurs before the company advertises the opening.

Consider this from the employer's perspective. If you were a hiring manager at a law firm and had several trusted employees, would you spend thousands of dollars advertising an associate position, sift through hundreds of résumés, conduct several hours of interviews, and then hire someone you do not know with the hope that this new person will be a model employee?

---

1. CAREERSHIFTERS, *Why The Best Jobs Are Never Advertised and How to Find Them*, http://www.careershifters.org/expert-advice/why-the-best-jobs-are-never-adverti sed-and-how-to-find-them (last visited Mar. 24, 2014).

Or would you prefer to interview candidates referred to you by trusted friends and colleagues who have put their reputations on the line by referring candidates to you?

How to Network

You walk into a networking reception or continuing education event and strike up a conversation with a lawyer standing next to you. Can you quickly let the person know who you are and what your career interests are? If you have not developed the ability to do this, it is important that you do so and get good at communicating it. By developing a 30-second "elevator" speech, you will sound like someone who has a plan and knows what he or she wants in his or her career. A good elevator speech includes the following:

1. Relevant background information, including education and experience;
2. A summary of your career interests; and
3. A question about the lawyer's practice area or career path.

Here is an example:

I am an attorney currently practicing general corporate and transactional law for a midsize firm. I really enjoy my practice, but I am interested in refocusing my career in the health law field. I have gone to several bar association events focused on health law, and I really enjoyed them. As a health law attorney, what experiences do you feel helped you to prepare for your law practice?

Assessing Your Network

Before contacting anyone, begin by assessing your personal network. Think about all of the people you know (friends, family, classmates, former employers or coworkers, community figures, acquaintances from your place of worship, past or current professors, etc.). Let the people in your network know about your interests. Ask them who they suggest you talk with to learn more about the field you are interested in. Contacts are often very willing to provide information and share their expertise with others. People enjoy discussing themselves and their work, especially with novices in the field.

Beyond your own personal network, there are numerous resources that will help you expand your network. Research alumni of your law school who practice in the area of health law. Join bar associations and read legal newspapers, magazines, and journals about what is going on in the local legal community. Talk to faculty members and check out Martindale.com, Lexis/Nexis, and Westlaw's career websites. Then, scour organization/firm websites for bios on the attorneys who work at firms with a position opening. Find a graduate of your law school or undergraduate institution. Look for an alum in the city you hope to move to. Talk to your office of career services for ideas. Look for someone you have a connection to, because she or he will likely be more willing to help you.

Expanding Your Network

The larger your network—the more people vested in your success—the more likely you are to find a desirable position. Key tips to grow your network are set forth here.

Develop Association Memberships

At every stage in an attorney's career, association membership is an important tool for networking and continuing education in his or her field. When you are in the process of job searching or transitioning into a new area of legal practice, membership in the right associations can be critical. Association membership provides excellent networking, mentoring, scholarship, and employment opportunities. In addition to providing many educational opportunities to help with health law skill mastery, associations provide ongoing coverage of developments in the field and breaking news. Additionally, membership in these associations demonstrates your involvement in the health law bar and community, which is critical for your résumé. Here is a list of health law associations to consider joining or becoming more involved in:

- American Bar Association Health Law Section
- American Health Lawyers Association
- State bar associations dedicated to health law
- State bar association health law sections

- City bar association health law sections
- Health Care Compliance Association
- American Health Information Management Association

Contact College and Law School Professors, Alumni Groups, and Career Services Offices

Get in touch with people already in your network, including your under-graduate and law school professors, especially those who teach in the health or health law area. Reach out to undergraduate and law school classmates by contacting your university's alumni office and registering with its alumni network. Classmates you were once close to, but whom you have not talked to in a while, will welcome your outreach. You never know where they may be working or who they may know that can help you with your job search. Not only is it nice to catch up, but they may work for a company or organization of interest to you.

Identify Law Firms and Other Organizations That Have a Health Law Focus

Perform Internet searches for law firms and organizations in your area that have a health law focus. In Chapter 3, we outlined many health law practice settings. Review the bios of attorneys at the firms or organizations you would like to work for. After reviewing the organization's website and reviewing attorneys' bios, reach out to attorneys at organizations where you would like to work and ask for informational meetings (informational meetings are discussed later in this chapter).

Use Social Media to Create an Online Presence

LinkedIn is the social media tool used most often by legal professionals. Recruiting firms, career coaches, law firm recruiters, and companies use it more than any other resource to find talent. Think of your LinkedIn profile as your online résumé. Create an effective LinkedIn profile by including a professional looking photo of yourself and creating a summary of your work experience and skills. Include any volunteer work you have done that shows you possess other transferable skills you may not have gained through employment. Also in your profile, list any articles you have pub-lished, certifications you have completed, honors you have received, and languages that you speak. The summary portion of your LinkedIn profile is a great place to showcase your experience and objectives.

Volunteer

Find a cause you are passionate about and volunteer. Donating your time to nonprofits and public interest organizations can help you develop lasting relationships with lawyers and other professionals. Volunteering at any organization is a good way to expand your network, but volunteering at an organization connected to health care can lead to meaningful connections in your chosen field.

Take Up a New Group Hobby

Taking up a new hobby will put you in touch with new groups of people with whom you share a common passion or skill. Taking up a group hobby can be an effective networking experience because the people you meet will have shared experiences. Done the right way, pursuing a new hobby is a very positive and rewarding experience that offers a chance for you and others to refine a skill and build relationships.

Attend Continuing Legal Education Programs

Most jurisdictions require lawyers to earn continuing legal education (CLE) credits throughout the year to maintain membership in the state bar. Approach CLE programs as opportunities to re-connect with alumni and get to know lawyers you don't currently know. Be strategic about the types of CLE programs you attend and make sure to register for those that relate to health law.

Informational Meetings

Informational meetings provide an excellent opportunity to learn about a person's career path and practice area. They can provide you with firsthand knowledge from people who know the inside scoop about a practice area. Informational meetings can help you prepare for job interviews because they require you to meet with practicing lawyers to discuss the legal profession, which will make you more comfortable in traditional interviews. Informational meetings can help you determine whether your strengths and personality are well suited to a specific content area or practice setting. They can make you a more impressive job candidate by revealing what is important to lawyers who practice in that area or who know what the employer is seeking in a candidate. The structure of the informational interview is one in which you ask the majority of the questions and direct the course of the discussion, as opposed to the job interview in which you are answering questions about yourself.

Setting Up the Meeting

Using e-mail to reach out for a meeting is the most appropriate and often the most expeditious way to reach your contact. Make sure when reaching out that you immediately state your connection to the contact. For example, state that you are an alumnus of the same institution (or whatever connection you have to the person). If someone has referred you to the person you are contacting, be sure to include that information up front. However, not having a connection with a potential contact should not dissuade you from reaching out to someone you would like to meet.

For example, the mere fact that the person has a health law practice and you are interested in learning more about it or that he or she practices in a four-attorney firm and you are interested in learning more about small firm practice is sufficient. In these instances, starting your e-mail with the following can be effective: *"I really want to learn more about your health law practice and the career path that you took,"* or *"I'd really appreciate any advice you have for a student interested in health law and how to best market myself in a down economy,"* or *"I'd love to get your thoughts on the firms in Chicago that are doing the best work in health law."*

Examples of What to Say on the Phone or in an E-mail
Example telephone call script:

> "Mr. Jones, my name is _____. I am a 1L/2L/3L at [law school], and I was given your name by _____. I understand that you practice in the area of _____, and I am very interested in learning more about that field. I'm looking for some general information and

wonder if you might have 15 minutes for me to drop by your office. I'd love to hear your advice and ideas for a student in my position."

Example e-mail script:

Dear Ms. Jones:
I am a 1L/2L/3L at [law school], and I was referred to you by Professor _____ when she learned of my interest in health law. I am very interested in the field and would love to get your insight on how to make myself most marketable to firms with a strong health law practice. If you could spare 15 minutes for a brief meeting in your office or a phone call at your convenience, I would appreciate the opportunity to get your advice for a student in my position. Please let me know if there is a convenient time to reach you, and I will follow up by phone next week.
Sincerely,
Susan Student

Follow up via a telephone call within 72 hours to try to schedule a meeting.

Be Prepared to Talk When You Call

When you call, your contact may answer the phone and say, "I have ten minutes right now, let's talk," so be prepared to have the conversation right then. Otherwise, ask your contact when it would be convenient for you to meet at his or her office. All correspondence, whether in letter or e-mail format, must be professional, grammatically correct, and typo free. Proofread!

Be Prepared to Introduce Yourself

Introducing yourself properly is often overlooked. It is something law students and lawyers forget to do because it seems so obvious. A brief introduction will quickly and clearly inform the person you are speaking to who you are, what your education and work history is, and what you are seeking. If you stumble through an explanation of who you are, what you have done, and where you want to go, your contact will find it more difficult to know what might be a good fit for you or whom to put you in contact with. Do not make it unnecessarily difficult for your networking contacts to know who you are and what you want. Only by revealing specifics about your background and interests will they know how to help you.

Be Prepared with a List of Questions to Ask

Prepare a list of questions to ask about the person's practice, organization, and career path, how the person sees his or her job changing and developing in the future, and what types of classes and internships he or she would recommend (see the list of questions in the following section). Make sure your résumé is updated and proofread so you can provide it immediately should your contact request it.

Conducting the Meeting

Your goal is to gather information, which means you need to be prepared to ask questions. In other words, it is up to you to direct the discussion. Your goal is to acquire basic information and impressions about work responsibilities, lifestyles, working conditions, educational and experience requirements, and the like. Remember that the informational meeting should be a low-stress, enjoyable conversation.

What to Discuss

Introduce yourself and express your appreciation that the contact is taking time to talk with you. Recognize that the person's time is valuable and that you do not want to take up too much of it. Continue to develop rapport by asking the contact to tell you about her or his position, personal career development, and likes and dislikes about the field.

Suggested Questions to Ask Your Networking Contact

Design your questions by first considering what you want to know. Your first informational meetings may be fairly general. As the search continues, you will ask more sophisticated questions about how to find a job in a particular market. Any of the questions that follow will provide you with useful information.

- How did you become interested in this area of the law?
- What part of your job provides the most challenges?
- What changes have you seen in your practice area over the years?
- How do you acquire clients (if in private practice)?
- Are there any lifestyle considerations I should be aware of?
- If you could start all over again, would you choose the same path?
- Are there any personal attributes that you feel are crucial to success in this field?
- What kinds of course work, additional training, and practical experiences will make me most marketable in your field?
- What do you think of my experiences to date? How can I improve my experience and résumé?
- Are there any professional organizations or publications that I should look into to learn more about the field?

End the interview with expressions of thanks for the contact's time and candor. As you near the end of the discussion, say, "You have been very helpful. Thank you so much for taking the time to speak with me. Is there anyone else you would suggest I talk to about practicing health law? May I say that you suggested I call?" Ask for permission to stay in touch to inquire about new developments and future leads.

Following Up After the Meeting
Always Send a Thank-You
After calling or meeting your contact, send a thank-you note or e-mail right away. Explain how much you appreciate the referrals and let your contact know that you'll be in touch from time to time.

Evaluate and Follow Through
Important final steps are to evaluate the information that you have gathered and to follow up on any leads that you have been given. Ask yourself these questions: What positive and negative impressions do I now have about the practice area/setting? How did this interview help me to clarify my career objectives? What more do I want to learn about this practice area/setting? What are my next steps? After each informational interview, you should

also make notes about your conversation to follow up on each lead and suggestion you were given. If you were given additional names of attorneys practicing in the field, follow up with them. It would be embarrassing for a contact to refer "a really terrific law student" to a friend—and that really terrific law student never bothered to call. If a contact suggested groups to join or publications to read, make sure you check them out. Following up on the suggestions you were given will also create opportunities to get back in touch with your contact to say thank you—for a personal referral that turned into a job offer, for a book recommendation that you found particularly helpful in your job search, and the like.

Keeping Track of Networking Contacts

Keep track of the people with whom you network by using Access, Excel, a three-ring binder, or note cards. Record your contact's name, contact information, employer, notes, follow-up, and date of last contact. On the back of any business cards that you receive, write down where you met each networking contact. It is also a good idea to connect with networking contacts on LinkedIn so that you can stay in touch long term and view others with whom your contacts are connected.

Etiquette and Other Considerations

- Make at least one or two new contacts each month. Remember that looking for a job is very time consuming, so set time aside each week to conduct your search.
- Do not demand too much time—many of your networking contacts will have tight schedules.
- Talk to your professors about their area—they can be important links on your network chain.
- Do not ask for a job or an internship—just ask for information in order to build the relationship.
- Follow up promptly on referrals.
- Contact people by their preferred method of contact.
- Prepare a telephone script and proofread your e-mail before making contact.

- Don't give up—you may need to try two or three times to reach the contact.
- Keep confidences—do not share sensitive information a contact may reveal to you.
- Keep your relationship with your contact alive by periodically checking in and updating him or her.
- Send a thank-you card or letter to let your contact know how her or his counsel has been valuable.
- Networking is a two-way street—if you see or read information your contact might find useful, share it with him or her.

For Law Students

While you have a wonderful opportunity in law school to take courses in a wide variety of subject matters—and you should—you need to also be strategic so that your resume presents a logical, coherent story to a potential employer. Next we discuss special considerations for law students preparing for a career in health law.

Master Basic Legal Skills

The primary goal of a legal education is to prepare you for a successful legal career. Using your time in law school strategically will give you a leg up on the competition. Legal employers seek candidates with strong research and writing experience, organizational and administrative skills, and good interpersonal and problem-solving skills. Cultivating these basic legal skills through course work, practical experience, and extracurricular activities is important to your professional success. Demonstrating your mastery of these important legal skills through your résumé, cover letter, writing sample, and interviews is essential to landing the job you want. Whether or not your law school offers an extensive health law curriculum, mastering basic legal skills is essential to finding a job in health law and succeeding once you are hired. Never lose sight of the importance of mastering the basics.

Go Beyond the Basics

Developing specific health law legal skills while in law school is an excellent way to set yourself apart from other job applicants and prepare you for the practice of health law. Some law schools have a strong health law program where students have the opportunity to take specialized classes that provide extensive study of specific areas of health law. Most law schools offer at least an introductory course in health law. The accompanying chart outlines the essential set of health law skills as defined by Loyola University Chicago School of Law's curriculum committee. This chart was designed to help students track their skill development and market those skills to potential employers.

Basic Health Law Skills	
General Lawyering Skills • Locate and analyze sources of health law; spot health law issues in case studies and transactions • Draft formal and informal legal analysis for attorney and non-attorney audiences • Work in groups to present; experience rating peers in group exercises • Experience drafting legal documents and interacting with clients **Understanding the Health Care Industry** • Comprehend the business, public policy, and regulatory environments governing health care • Spot key operational and legal issues faced by health care entities • Identify issues in organizational documents; draft analysis of legal issues • Familiar with corporate and non-profit structures, tax exemption issues, and financial statements and forms • Understand creation of health care entities, including selection of corporate form; basic organizational documents; identify governance duties and conflicts of interest • Analyze tax exemption issues, financing options, and the role of private investment	**Hospitals and Health Care Systems** • Interpret right-to-care situations; identify underserved populations and strategies to improve access • Aware of informed consent and EMTALA; able to spot basic patient rights issues and propose solutions • Explain models for delivery and payment; familiar with facility policies and medical staff bylaws; awareness of accreditation standards and processes **Health Care Payment Systems** • Knowledge of licensing laws, procedures, and processes • Recognition of federal and state roles in regulating health care • Analyze anti-kickback statute, Stark, false claims, anti-competitive conduct, and basic compliance policies

---

Specialty Skills

Health Care Payment Systems
- Describe payor types; understand federal and state laws regulating Medicare and Medicaid
- Navigate the payor contracting process; analyze key contract provisions between insurers and providers

Health Information and Technology
- Interpret basic federal laws, including HIPAA
- Understand basic laws and issues related to electronic medical records

Health Care Litigation
- Appreciate the basic duties of health care providers, negligence, standard of care, causation, and types of damage awards; able to draft analysis of hypotheticals based on existing case law

Life Sciences
- Explain the FDA's role and processes
- Familiar with and ability to draft analysis of the role of clinical research and processes, genomics and personalized medicine, and the FCPA

Public Interest
- Adept in assisting uninsured and medically underserved patients
- Ability to provide legal advice and referrals on legal and social issues
- Familiar with cases, statutes, and legal doctrines relating to the rights, treatment, and incarceration of mentally ill and developmentally disabled persons

---

Gain Practical Experience

Regardless of what concentration you ultimately pursue, practical experience is an integral part of a legal education and an important preparation for a career as an attorney. Participation also signals to potential employers your commitment to the field and your ability to balance extracurricular and academic interests. In Chapter 3, we discuss places where you can work as a health lawyer. Many of the practice settings listed in Chapter 3 are excellent places to look for an externship or part-time job while you are still a student.

Part-Time Employment

Many law students work as part-time law clerks or summer associates at law firms with health law practice groups, or they clerk for a judge. As the legal job market has become more competitive, practical experience has become increasingly important. It is no longer enough to graduate with an impressive GPA; employers are looking for real-world experience and a familiarity with the actual practice of law.

The first thing you should do when looking for a part-time job is to talk to your network of family and friends and find out if they have connections in the legal community. Many part-time employment opportunities are also advertised through law school career services offices. Make sure that your professors, student advisors, and career services advisors know that you are interested in part-time work so that they can inform you of opportunities. Follow up on all leads promptly, and do not be afraid to pick up the phone instead of waiting for an e-mail reply. It is never too early to start networking.

Externships

Another way to develop health law skills and résumé credentials is through externships approved by your law school. Externships are opportunities for law students to gain practical experience outside the classroom while earning law school credit. Students work off-campus under the supervision of attorneys or judges. Law students often extern at hospitals, trade associations, or government agencies. The following are examples of organizations that often have legal externs:

- Medical, practitioner, and other trade associations
- State hospital associations
- Hospitals and health care systems
- U.S. Department of Health and Human Services
- Centers for Medicare and Medicaid Services
- State and local departments of public health
- State office of attorney general
- Office of Inspector General

Depending on the site of your externship, your experience will vary greatly. Overall, externships are generally research and writing intensive. Having an externship is a great way to develop an impressive writing sample that you can use when applying for jobs in the future. It is also an excellent way to network with health law attorneys and other professionals. Check with your law school about its externship application process and a list of approved externship sites.

Clinical Experience

Participating in a clinic affords students the opportunity to engage in legal practice while still in law school. Clinics offer law students a unique opportunity to take ownership over their caseload. In a clinic, as opposed to other types of experiential learning opportunities, law students are responsible for developing their own cases, rather than executing case plans designed by a supervisor.

Students develop and implement their case plans under the supervision of clinical faculty. With the guidance of faculty, clinic students connect theory and practice to hone lawyering skills critical to careers in health law.[2] For example, courses offered through the Health Justice Project, a medical-legal partnership clinic at Loyola University Chicago School of Law, focus on the "development of skills in interdisciplinary practice, client interviewing and counseling, fact finding and analysis, legal research and document drafting, pursuit of administrative and other legal remedies, policy advocacy and reform where appropriate, and creative problem solving for the benefit of clients."[3]

For students interested in careers in health law, opportunities to participate in interdisciplinary clinics are particularly valuable. Interdisciplinary collaboration, such as working with health services professionals and/or patients/consumers, permeates all aspects of health law. Therefore, aspiring health law leaders should enroll in clinics that will give them the opportunity to acquire these skills.

In addition to cultivating skills necessary for effective legal practice, clinics provide law students with the opportunity to expand access to justice by providing legal services to underserved individuals. In most clinics, students work for the benefit of low-income clients who may not otherwise have access to the legal system. Health law students work to provide these clients, and the community, with improved health outcomes and social conditions.

---

2. Emily A. Benfer, *Educating the Next Generation of Health Leaders: Medical-Legal Partnership and Interdisciplinary Graduate Education*, J. LEGAL MED. (forthcoming Spring 2014).

3. BEAZLEY INST. FOR HEALTH LAW AND POLICY, *Course Offerings and Student Opportunities*, http://luc.edu/law/centers/healthlaw/hjp/course_students.html (last visited Mar. 24, 2014).

Many students regard participation in a clinic as one of the most rewarding and memorable experiences they have in law school. Participating in clinics will help law students set themselves apart from their peers when beginning their careers in health law.

Extracurricular Activities

Extracurricular activities offer opportunities to learn about health law and become involved in the community outside the classroom. Your law school may have a health law student group. If your school does not have a health law group, you may consider inviting health law speakers through another student organization, the student bar association, for example. Participating in your school's health law journal or contributing an article on a topic related to health law to another law journal is a great way to engage with health law subject matter and show employers that this is an area of interest for you.

Health law experiences outside law school are also beneficial to students pursuing careers in the field. They provide educational enhancement and important networking opportunities with national and local professionals. Participating in a health law moot court competition or other health law competition is a great way to learn and network. Here are a few health law competitions you might consider competing in:

- Loyola University Chicago School of Law Health Law Transactional Competition
- University of Maryland Law School's annual Health Law and Regulatory Compliance competition
- American College of Legal Medicine National Health Law Moot Court Competition

There are also a number of health law writing contests open to law students. Noteworthy health law writing competitions include the following:

- ABA Health Law Section's Writing Competition
- Epstein, Becker and Green Annual Health Law Writing Competition
- American College of Legal Medicine Writing Competition

- The Food and Drug Law Institute H. Thomas Austern Memorial Writing Competition
- American Society for Pharmacy Law Larry M. Simonsmeier Writing Award

Other health law opportunities may include assisting a faculty member with a health law–related research project or participating in a health law–focused study abroad program. The following is a list of health law study abroad programs:

- Seton Hall
  - Study Law in Europe Program in Belgium and Switzerland
- Harvard
  - HSPH Health Reform and Community Medicine Course in Chile
  - Collaborative Public Health Field Course in Brazil
- University of Virginia
  - January Term Abroad in Tel Aviv examining the Israeli Health System
- University of Maryland
  - World Health Organization Externship Program
- St. Louis University
  - Semester in Ireland examining Medical Law

For Lawyers Transitioning to Health Law or Changing Paths within Health Law

In addition to the educational competencies, membership association, and certifications mentioned earlier in this chapter, other opportunities are available to lawyers seeking to change their career path.

Advanced Degrees

One way for a lawyer who wishes to transition to health law or change paths within health law to make him- or herself more marketable is to pursue an advanced degree. Following are descriptions of six advanced degrees that allow lawyers to expand upon existing specializations or develop new ones. Pursuing an advanced degree may be particularly helpful for lawyers who attended law schools that do not have a large health law program.

Master of Laws (LLM)

Master of Laws (LLM) is a post–Juris Doctor master's degree for attorneys who wish to develop a special expertise in health law. LLM programs are generally one-year full-time or two-year part-time programs that culminate with a thesis paper on a health law topic. During the course of the program, students will take only advanced classes within the health law specialization. Some LLM programs also have an experiential component in which students will extern in different health law practice settings in addition to completing health law course work.

Although other advanced degrees, discussed later in this chapter, may be of significant value to advancing your career goals, the LLM degree is the only one that focuses on furthering your understanding of law as it impacts the health care field.

CAREER PROFILE

William D. Smart Jr.
Assistant General Counsel
Advocate Health Care

I am an Assistant General Counsel in the Legal Department of Advocate Health Care (Advocate). By most measures, Advocate is the largest health care system in the state of Illinois. In addition to the 11 Advocate hospitals, Advocate Medical Group employs more than 1,200 physicians. I work in Advocate's corporate headquarters in Downers Grove, Illinois.

I made my decision to pursue a career in health law in 2011. Unfortunately, the closely held real estate developer for whom I served as general counsel was a casualty of the commercial real estate crisis. Given the dearth of opportunities for real estate counsel in 2011, I felt that I needed to take my career in an entirely new direction. A combination of the headlines generated by the Affordable Care Act and an interest in the health care marketplace developed from a variety of life experiences led me to enroll in the Master of Laws in Health Law program at Loyola University

Continued

CAREER PROFILE *Continued*

Chicago School of Law in January 2011. I received my LLM in January 2013—28 years after I had received my Juris Doctor from the University of Illinois College of Law.

Loyola allowed me to take a combination of online and on-campus courses. That flexibility allowed me to pursue my LLM as a stay-at-home dad while my wife continued her career as an attorney at a Chicago law firm. Frankly, I found that I was a much better law student the second time around because the more targeted subject matter was intellectually compelling and I had a better understanding of my ultimate goal. The perspective gained during my years as a practicing lawyer helped me to succeed as a student as well.

As part of the Loyola LLM program, I was an extern in the Advocate Legal Department during the 2012 spring term. I returned to Advocate six months later in November 2012—this time as an employee—for the primary purpose of assisting with the due diligence process in connection with the affiliation between Advocate and a single-hospital health system. After the affiliation transaction was completed, I continued to work on a variety of matters, including a number of physician practice acquisitions. In January 2013, I became an Assistant General Counsel. In addition to continuing my work on transactional matters, I have a number of other responsibilities, including primary responsibility for providing legal support to one of Advocate's hospitals.

I am very pleased with my transition from real estate counsel to health care attorney. I am able to put my transactional experience to good use while I take advantage of what I learned through Loyola's LLM program. Even more important to me is that I am able to tap into the collective health law experience of the Advocate Legal Department to address whatever legal challenges may be presented. This vast wealth of legal experience allows for creative solutions and approaches to today's legal issues. In addition, and more important to me, the Legal Department's storehouse of legal acumen will help design and implement the solutions to tomorrow's legal challenges in the rapidly evolving health care marketplace.

Master of Public Health (MPH)

Master of Public Health (MPH) is a master's degree that focuses on promoting the health of the overall population. Public health law "involves laws and policies intended to prevent health problems and promote health across the population, while health or health care law involves legal concerns related to the medical treatment of individuals."[4] An MPH is a helpful degree for lawyers who want to learn about population health, ethics, and health interventions as well as about quantitative methods in classes such as epidemiology and biostatistics.[5] The following tracks are the general areas of study for public health:

- Health Policy and Management
- Social and Behavioral Sciences
- Biostatistics
- Environmental Health Science
- Epidemiology

Master of Public Administration (MPA)/Public Policy (MPP)

Master of Public Administration (MPA) is a master's degree program that prepares students for careers in public service and nonprofit management. The MPA degree aims to teach students the principles of public administration, public policy management, and policy implementation. A similar and complimentary degree to the MPA is the Master of Public Policy (MPP). MPP degree programs provide students with the skills necessary to analyze policy and evaluate programs in political and managerial roles. This degree places an emphasis on creating "highly-skilled, well-trained policy analysts who can dissect a problem, analyze and interpret data, and evaluate and create alternative courses of action."[6] The skills gained from an MPP degree function in a variety of settings from government to nonprofit and private employers, domestically and internationally.

Master of Health Administration (MHA)

Master of Health Administration (MHA) is a master's degree program designed for those students who wish to work in hospitals, consulting

---

4. Network for Public Health Law, Public Health Law Careers Fact Sheet, http://www.networkforphl.org/_asset/zjk2ng/Public-Health-Law-Career-Paths-FINAL.pdf (last visited Mar. 24, 2014).

5. *Id.*

6. Georgetown Univ. McCourt School of Pub. Policy, *Master of Public Policy*, http://gppi.georgetown.edu/academics/mpp/ (last visited Mar. 24, 2014).

firms, and other health care–related businesses. MHA programs have a curriculum that generally includes the study of economics, policy, public health, and other aspects of the U.S. health care system as well as managerial skills. Often, there is an overlap in skills taught in MHA and Master of Business Administration (MBA) programs, so careful review of offered curriculums should be undertaken to determine differences important to you.

Master of Health Science (MHS)

The Master of Health Sciences (MHS) is a master's degree program that generally takes one of two approaches. Some MHS programs are designed for those students who wish to work in academic or research roles in the health science field, while others are designed for those who wish to advance their career in public health. Schools often offer MHS degrees through several of their programs in order to allow for specialization of the curriculum. Core courses for all MHS degree programs include research methods and analysis, evidence-based literature review, and courses on trends in health care delivery and health policy.

Master of Business Administration (MBA)

Some Master of Business Administration (MBA) programs focus on business management in the health care industry. MBA programs offer a curriculum focused on leadership and analytics. All MBA programs focus on the basics of business management. MBA programs with a health care focus provide the latest practical applications of business skills in health care management. These programs are designed to give students the knowledge, skill, and understanding to successfully manage and lead in the health care industry.

Certifications

Another way to gain substantive knowledge in health law areas and to make yourself a more competitive job applicant is to receive a certification from an association or university. This can be beneficial for law students and practicing attorneys alike. Compliance is an area of health care in which an additional certification is common and often required for employment. The Health Care Compliance Association offers seven different compliance certifications, including a general certification in health care compliance and a certification in research compliance. Various law schools also offer certification opportunities.

Continuing Legal Education

To bolster your résumé and learn new skills without investing in an advanced degree or certification, you might consider continuing legal education opportunities. Most bar associations offer webinars, in-person programs, audio downloads, and online classes. Look for local, state, and national opportunities to complete continuing legal education (CLE) programs on health law topics.

Pro Bono Work

Many organizations provide pro bono opportunities for attorneys to gain practical experience in health law. Attorneys interested in performing these types of services should seek out public interest organizations and initiatives that provide legal representation in health-related areas. Typical opportunities for representing clients include access to health care, medical malpractice claims, obtaining insurance and other benefits, Social Security benefits, and medical debt collection. Representing pro bono clients in these areas enables attorneys to better understand the health care delivery system while demonstrating their interest in the field.

Marketing Legal Skills for Nonlegal Jobs

Attorneys possess many skills that can be marketed in nonlegal jobs. In health-related nonlegal jobs, knowledge of the industry is still quite important. Additionally, lawyers should focus on many of the skills they possess, including critical thinking and analysis, research and writing, problem solving, applying theory, editing and proofreading, handling stressful situations and deadlines effectively, communicating with clients, resolving conflicts, and working well without supervision.[7] Many attorneys with practice experience

---

7. LEGAL AUTHORITY, *Breaking Away From the Norm—Nontraditional and Non-Legal Careers*, *available at* http://www.legalauthority.com/articles/pdf/70107.pdf.

are comfortable working as part of a team, leading and mentoring others, and overseeing complex and detailed projects on tight deadlines. These skills are very marketable outside the legal industry. By focusing on their leadership skills and combining these with knowledge of an industry, attorneys are able to pursue opportunities outside the traditional legal realm. Chapter 4 details alternative opportunities within the field of health law.

CAREER PROFILE

Drew McCormick
Associate General Counsel
Rush University Medical Center in Chicago

I began my career in the fall of 2011 as an associate in the health care department at McGuireWoods LLP, which is a 900-lawyer, multinational law firm. As a junior attorney at a large law firm, I had tremendous resources at my fingertips, including incredibly knowledgeable colleagues and mentors. I believe that early training at a large firm was a key advantage in the development of my legal skills that will continue to enhance my marketability throughout my career.

Although I received excellent training at McGuireWoods, I desired to shift my practice to an in-house position for a variety of reasons. First, I was attracted to the notion of being dedicated to serving a single client and becoming deeply integrated within that client. Second, I feel a strong passion for serving a mission-based, not-for-profit organization that contributes appreciable value to the Chicago community. Third, working for a large academic medical center provides me with the opportunity to expand my legal practice to include other related areas of interest, including risk management, patient safety, and bioethics.

In my position as an Associate General Counsel in the Office of Legal Affairs at Rush University Medical Center in Chicago (Rush), each day is dynamic and full of new and exciting challenges. I touch multiple substantive legal areas every day. I also have a great deal of variety in terms of the mechanisms for providing legal services, including not only writing memoranda and performing legal research but also participating in meetings to provide guidance to medical center leaders, handling project management, performing training and education, developing and revising institutional policy, and carrying out analytical problem solving.

On any given day at Rush, I attend several meetings on a variety of topics, including committee meetings, collaboration with colleagues in risk management and compliance regarding new questions or ongoing projects, and interactions with business or clinical personnel to discuss a variety of regulatory issues, strategic initiatives, and transactions. I also spend a significant amount of my time researching key regulatory issues in areas such as fraud and abuse, health information privacy, clinical research, reimbursement, and a variety of other areas. In addition, I draft and revise policies, contracts, consent forms, and other key legal documents related to the operation of the medical center.

When I was a law student and firm lawyer, I was told that in-house work is often mundane and that only firm attorneys enjoy interesting, "cutting-edge" projects. Since starting at Rush in October 2013, I have found this to be entirely inconsistent with my experience. A key distinction between firm and in-house practice is that the business model of a law firm often pushes attorneys into niche specialization. This enables the law firm to offer its clients highly specialized expertise in a variety of substantive legal areas. Now that I am a consumer of those services, I appreciate being able to draw on such expertise. However, though this is a successful business model for a law firm, my personal experience is that this approach makes it difficult for an individual with a variety of interests to develop multiple skill sets and a broad legal knowledge base.

In my short tenure at Rush, I have already confronted many difficult and fascinating legal issues at the forefront of the evolving health care industry. I have found this to be very challenging at times, but equally rewarding. It is exciting be a part of the continuing revolution of health care in America and incredibly fulfilling to help facilitate the provision of top-quality care to the patients that rely on Rush. I am honored and privileged to serve Rush as in-house counsel.

Chapter 6

Applying for Jobs in Health Law

After you have completed the essential preliminary steps outlined in Chapter 5, you will be ready to begin applying for jobs in health law. This chapter is especially helpful for new graduates who are applying for law jobs for the first time. In this chapter, we will give you the tools to create a strong résumé that will lead to interviews. We will then provide advice on how to have a successful interview and land the job you want.

Preparing Your Health Law Résumé

A résumé is a marketing piece and often your first point of contact with potential employers. Applicants are surprised to learn that employers often take less than a minute to review a résumé, so it is important to make every word count. Your résumé should be appealing to the eye and easy to read and should contain information a legal employer wants to read. Put yourself in the shoes of the reader. Do not assume the reader will know what you mean. It is essential to be specific and clear. Please see Appendix F for sample résumés.

To begin the process of creating a health law résumé, make a list of (1) everything you have done since high school graduation, including your education, jobs, volunteer work, achievements, awards, internships, hobbies, and language skills; (2) any relevant legal experience you have acquired prior to, during, and after law school; (3) any research and writing skills you have acquired; and (4) other skills and work experience you have acquired, including leadership, team work, public speaking, prior health care employment, and volunteer work.

Create an easy-to-read résumé by using a simple font such as Times New Roman, Arial, or Century Schoolbook in 12-point size. Use bold, italic, or underline commands to emphasize information and to create interest and variation. Margins should be approximately one inch on all sides; text should be single spaced. As a rule, the length should not exceed one page.

Your name, address, phone number, and e-mail address should appear at the top of the page and should be centered. Your e-mail address should be professional and one that you check often. Other sections of your résumé should include Education, Experience, and, if pertinent, Bar Admissions, Volunteer Work, and/or Special Skills.

Law students and new graduates should list their education first, then their work experience, and so on. Lawyers who have acquired postgraduate work experience should list their experience first and then their education. In either case, list your education and your work experience in reverse chronological order (most recent first).

Education

Information to list in your education section includes the degree you received (Juris Doctor, LLM, etc.), your graduation dates, any honors and scholarships you received, activities you engaged in, and organizations you joined. A published paper in a legal journal or other legal publication should be cited completely. If you have written extensively on a subject, consider creating a separate section titled Publications on your résumé, but only if relevant to health law employers. Course work is generally not necessary to list. However, if you took numerous health law courses in or after law school or completed any relevant certifications, highlight them by including them on your résumé. Opinions differ on the subject, but your grade point average (GPA) and class rank should be included on your résumé if it is above 3.0 and you are a law student or new attorney. As you advance in your career, your GPA and class rank can be left off your résumé as they become less and less relevant.

Work Experience

List paid and unpaid work in reverse chronology, with your most recent job listed first. Include all relevant full-time and part-time legal jobs, clinical work, externships, internships, research assistantships, volunteer legal work, and any relevant nonlegal work experience. Include each employer's name, city, and state, your dates of employment, and your title and job responsibilities and use bullet points when listing responsibilities to make reading easier. Lead with your most impressive achievements—not necessarily what you did most often—and remember to use active, not passive, language to describe accomplishments.

It is important to give yourself credit for the experience you have acquired. The way to do this is to be specific about your achievements at work. Discuss specific areas of law you researched and specific motions you wrote. For example, state that you "conducted legal research and wrote legal memoranda in a complex litigation case involving breach of a physician employment agreement" rather than "wrote legal memoranda." Be specific about the legal issues you addressed, the practice areas in which you worked, the laws you researched, and the actions that you took.

Include skills applicable to the practice of law, such as writing, analyzing, researching, organizing, arguing, advocating, public speaking, coordinating, creating, persuading, delegating, editing, assessing, estimating, planning, and supervising, and gear your résumé to the responsibilities the employer lists in the job description. If the job requires that you research and write, make sure to highlight your research and writing skills/experience and provide specific examples, such as "Wrote two motions for summary judgment, a motion to dismiss, three complaints, and discovery requests including interrogatories and correspondence."

Be sure to place special emphasis on any experiences or skills that relate to health law, including matters handled for health care clients, or on issues similar to those handled by health lawyers (e.g., tax exemption or insurance disputes).

If you did not come to law school directly from college, you need to account for the time in between, if possible. When describing what you did, highlight any law-related and health law transferable skills.

Describe any current job that you hold in the *present tense*. Describe past jobs in the *past tense*. If you held several positions with the same employer, list the employer's name and location once and underneath list each position with descriptions for each.

Special Skills/Interests

If relevant, you may want to add a special skills section to your résumé and include volunteer activities, pro bono work, licenses, professional associations, languages you speak, and so on. This information can communicate talents and personality traits that may not be apparent elsewhere on your résumé. Special skills and interests often show leadership qualities, social awareness, community involvement, and other attributes, which many employers seek in applicants. They may also provide a connection with the reader or a topic of conversation during the interview.

Preparing for the Interview

Legal employers look for candidates who appear professional, intelligent, enthusiastic, capable, hard-working, easy to get along with, and interested in the employer and what the employer does. Careful preparation for interviews is essential, because they involve a relatively short time in which to make a positive impression and distinguish yourself from other candidates. Before any interview, you should research the employer and identify areas of your background that make you a good fit for the position. Make sure that you highlight these experiences in the interview.

There are a number of steps every candidate should take to maximize the career opportunities that interviews represent. Careful preparation can set you up for a successful interview experience, no matter what background, prior interview experience, or comfort level you start with.

Good interview preparation involves much more than polishing your résumé and pressing your best suit. Preparing a résumé and preparing to talk about your résumé are two different things entirely. As you put together your résumé, you craft descriptions of your education, employment, and other activities. Talking about your résumé, on the other hand, means being thoroughly prepared to go into detail about every entry on your résumé and thinking of concise and easy-to-tell stories about every entry on your résumé that will emphasize your skills and experience for the legal position you are seeking.

You will also need to be prepared to talk about topics that are not covered by your résumé—for example, your plans for the future and professional goals. One of the most sensitive areas of interview preparation is thinking of creative ways to address any weaknesses in your résumé or candidacy. You will also need to research every employer you interview with and come up with a list of appropriate questions to ask during the interview.

Discussing Your Résumé in Interviews

You should be fully prepared to discuss any entry on your résumé in detail. If you have listed "drafted discovery requests" as a task you undertook as a law clerk, you may be asked, "What kinds of cases did you draft discovery for?" Be prepared to answer intelligently—for example, "I worked mostly on medical malpractice cases, so the interrogatories and document requests I drafted were largely about hospitals' practices and procedures." Similarly, be prepared to briefly summarize the key legal issues involved in any pleadings, briefs, or judicial opinions you mention having drafted.

Being prepared to go into detail also means that you should go back and read any legal memoranda or publications you list on your résumé, including your undergraduate or graduate thesis. If your interviewer is knowledgeable in the areas in which you have written or published, you want to be sure that you can hold your own on a topic you may not have thought about in a while.

Attire

Dress professionally and conservatively. Present a professional image by not carrying a backpack or oversized purse. Present yourself in the "uniform" that is appropriate for the organization. Even if everyday dress can be casual in the employer's workplace, present yourself as you would appear when representing the organization in a courtroom, client meeting, or other formal situation. Stick to classic looks and well-tailored pieces. Adding a vibrant color to an otherwise neutral outfit reads confident and can be more memorable.

What to Bring to the Interview

Bring at least five copies of your résumé, along with copies of your writing sample, transcript, and list of references. Do this even if you submitted the material in advance. You may meet new people who would be interested in seeing a copy, or the interviewer may have forgotten to bring his or her copy.

Logistics

Confirm where the interview will be held. Some organizations have more than one location. Print out detailed directions. Be generous in estimating the time you will need to arrive punctually. You should arrive at the location about ten minutes early. Never arrive late! Before you enter the offices, stop in a restroom to make one last inspection of your appearance. Be courteous to everyone, whether they are on the road, in the parking lot, on the street outside the building, or in the building itself. You never know who you will meet on your way to an interview, and any one of those people could be involved in making hiring decisions for the employer.

Nonverbal Communication

Throughout the interview, the employer will be studying your nonverbal communication skills and listening carefully to your responses. A firm handshake and direct eye contact are two of the most important nonverbal messages you can send to the employer. They indicate that you are confident, energetic, and sincerely interested in the employer. They illustrate how you will present yourself as a lawyer.

Answering Interview Questions

Interviewers have different styles, so it is hard to predict what kinds of questions you will be asked when you interview. Preparing for a wide variety of questions is the best way to head into any interview; you want to feel confident that you will be able to answer any question that comes your way. Review lists of interview questions and consider how you will answer each one, and then practice verbalizing those answers aloud. Thinking about what you want to say and actually verbalizing your answers out loud are two completely different things. Practicing answers aloud will ensure that your answers are well organized, concise, and articulate. It may take a lot of practice, but you want to go into an interview confident that you will be able to talk about your skills and experience in an engaging and articulate way.

The question behind every interview question an employer asks is "Why should we hire you?" Make it easy on potential employers by answering this question for them. Make sure that your answers express your interest in the practice of health law and the particular employer you are interviewing with. Give the interviewer concrete examples of your strengths, skills, and experience. Saying that you have "strong leadership skills" does not tell a potential employer much, but discussing a group, program, or project that you have led does. Make sure that your answers reflect the characteristics employers are looking for—good judgment, problem-solving skills, dedication, a strong work ethic, solid legal writing and reasoning skills, the ability to work independently, and the ability to get along with others.

You will want to have answers to common interview questions planned in advance. Of course, you do not want to answer questions in an interview as if you are reading from a script, but you do want to have thought of what you want to say ahead of time and tried your responses out by speaking them aloud—either to yourself, to a friend, or in a mock interview.

Interviews often begin with the question, "So tell me about yourself." Think carefully about how to answer this question as it can set the tone for the whole interview. A good answer is about one minute long and includes both some personal information (especially information that ties you to the geographic location of the employer and/or its practice areas) and some information about your professional goals. For example,

"I'm a transplant to Chicago, but I plan to live and work here after graduation. I was born and raised in Detroit, but I came to Chicago and worked as a health consultant here at Smith Consulting for four years after undergrad. I am especially interested in building on the experience I gained at X law school and at Smith Consulting. One of the reasons I'm so interested in Big Firm is that I have heard great things about your health law practice."

Negative Questions

Be aware that an employer may ask you to describe what you liked or did not like about your last job, fellow workers, or supervisor. These questions should be answered carefully so as not to identify yourself as a "problem employee." Even if you had an absolutely miserable experience at your last place of employment, say something positive and do not go into detail about any specific dissatisfaction or negative experience you may have had. Such a response is a flag for the employer and may prompt follow-up questions that change the focus of the interview entirely. Your goal is to be positive and upbeat throughout the interview. Do not allow yourself to be dragged into negative discussions.

Interview Questions You May Be Asked

The following questions are common ones that you may encounter during interviews. Develop concise, well-organized answers before you begin interviewing. Consider how each answer responds to the interviewer's unspoken question, "Why should we hire you?" Consider doing a mock interview with your career services office or with a friend or colleague before your interview.

- **Tell me about yourself.** Employers are looking for a one-minute-or-less, focused, concise statement about you, as if you were responding to the question "Why should we hire you?" Employers are looking for a statement that showcases your experience, career progress, major accomplishments, and some of your best traits and that casts you in a positive light.
- **Why are you interested in our firm/organization?** You should be able to articulate specifically what interests you about the organization. Look for facts: specific practice areas, actual clients, actual results (successful completion of the merger between client A and client B). Do not be satisfied with stating, "Your size, location, and breadth of practice areas."
- **Why are you interested in this geographic area? Do you have any ties to this community?** If you have lived/worked in the area, this is easy. If you have no ties to the area, you should refer to ties to nearby or similar places, visits to the area, or an interest in living and working in a large city/small town. Before your interview, you may want to talk to

classmates/friends who have lived and worked in the geographic area where you are seeking employment so that you can give details about events/places/neighborhoods if relevant.

- **What can I tell you about the firm?** Lead with something you know about the firm—for example, "I know that you recently expanded your health law practice group. What led to that decision?" This shows that you were interested enough in the employer to do some research to prepare for the interview.

- **Why are you interested in practicing health law?** Employers are looking for answers that make sense and that show you have good judgment. They do not want to hear that you are just looking for a job and you know that there are a lot of jobs in health law. Employers are looking for answers that show that you were thoughtful about your decision in choosing or changing your career path and that you researched the market and area of law and made a thoughtful, conscious choice.

- **Do you think your law school grades are a good indication of your abilities?** No matter what your grades are, you will need to go beyond grades to convey those skills that are essential to good lawyering. If your grades are strong, do not brag. Instead, go beyond your grades to talk about how much you have learned, the classes you have taken, and the experience you have gained. If your grades are weak, tell the interviewer the steps you have taken to improve your grades or other ways in which you have excelled during or after law school (law journal, moot court, as a law clerk or an associate at a law firm).

Questions to Ask Employers During an Interview

Employers will evaluate the depth of your interest in working at their organization by the nature of the questions you ask. Ask thoughtful questions that show that you are interested in the employer, have already researched the organization, and want to learn more. Do not ask questions that can be answered with simple research on, for example, the NALP (National Association for Law Placement) form, the organization's website, or a promotional brochure. Take your questions to greater depth—for example, "I saw that you recently published an article about the apparent agency of hospitals in medical malpractice lawsuits. Did your interest in the subject come out of cases you had worked on?"

Bear in mind that the questions you ask should differ depending on the type of job you are interviewing for. If you are interviewing for a part-time job during your first year that will likely not lead to postgraduate employment, confine your questions to the type of work the employer does, the type of work the employer will expect you to do, how you will be assigned work, and the work hours the employer expects. If you are interviewing for a full-time position to begin immediately, it is appropriate to ask more sophisticated, forward-looking questions.

- What is the law firm/corporation looking for in the ideal candidate?
- What type of work should I expect to do?
- Will the work be litigation or transactional in nature?
- How are work assignments distributed to associates?
- What types of legal writing assignments will I be given?
- Will I interact with all of the attorneys in the department?
- How much client interaction can I expect to have?
- What types of clients do you work with?

A great final question for employers is "What is the next step in the interview process?" This question is a good way to close the interview and find out if additional interviews will be necessary and how long the organizations may take to deliberate.

Behavioral Interviews

The theory behind behavioral interviewing is that past performance is a good predictor of future performance or behavior. Behavioral interviews ask questions that require applicants to describe how they behaved, made decisions, solved problems, and finished projects at work in the past. The interviewer typically identifies job-related competencies and then asks questions that help gauge whether you possess those competencies. For example, "Describe a time when you were faced with a stressful situation that demonstrated your coping skills" is considered a behavioral interview question because it asks the applicant to describe an event or situation that happened in the past to determine how that applicant might behave in a similar situation in the future. The best way to prepare for a behavioral interview is to arm yourself with examples and stories of previous challenges and successes.

Phone or Skype Interviews

Applicants today are more often being offered phone or Skype interviews, especially if they are interviewing with an employer that is out of town. The challenge in a phone or Skype interview is to establish rapport with the interviewer. If at all possible, try to conduct the phone interview on a land-line phone in order to avoid dropping the call in the middle of the interview. Conduct your telephone and Skype interviews in a quiet, calm, clean, and business-like setting. If you do your phone or Skype interview from home, do it when you are alone in the house and out of range of barking dogs and crying babies. Dress as you would for an in-person interview and have your résumé, the job description, some prepared answers to challenging questions, and information about the employer in front of you. Especially for telephone interviews, it is important to have polished answers to anticipated questions and to convey an energetic and enthusiastic tone. Also consider standing up during phone interviews, and for Skype interviews, remember to smile and look directly at the camera to make as much eye contact as possible.

Handling Group/Team Interviews

Group or team interviews offer candidates a chance to put group management and presentation skills on display. If possible, find out the names of the interviewers prior to the interview in order to know who will be a part of the interview. As quickly as possible, try to read the various personality types of the interviewers and find a way to adjust to and connect with them. Group interviews often allow each group member to ask interview questions. Make sure to make eye contact with the person asking the question and then with everyone else in the group. Group interviews can be stressful, which can cause you to respond to questions too quickly, so take a few seconds to think about your answers before responding to questions.

After the Interview

Immediately after the interview, write to the person or persons who interviewed you to thank them for taking the time to interview you. Remember to get a business card from each person you meet with so you know where to send the thank-you card or e-mail. Include references to details of your visit in your note.

Handwritten thank-you cards (if you have legible handwriting) are appropriate. If you have been communicating with the employer/interviewer by e-mail throughout the interview process, e-mail can also be appropriate for a thank-you. However, because of the natural tendency to be more casual in e-mails, make sure you proofread your thank-you e-mails thoroughly. Print out any e-mail and read it before sending to make sure your tone is appropriately professional.

Monitor Status Tactfully

Job offers are not usually made during the interview. If you do not hear from an employer within a reasonable time (seven to ten business days), you may e-mail or call to ask about the status of deliberations and ask if any additional information is needed from you.

Acknowledge Any Job Offer Immediately

If you receive a job offer, immediately affirm your interest and ask the date by which you are expected to respond. Most organizations have a timetable and expect you to respond, either with an acceptance or a rejection, by that date. Keep in mind that many employers expect quick responses, especially smaller offices eager to fill vacancies.

Respond to Job Offers Appropriately

Timing and tact are critical when you have received an offer and the employer wants a decision, but you may be waiting to hear about another job you would prefer. You can ask the first employer for an extension of the time by which they want your decision. Be careful how you present that request. Do not give the impression that the employer is a poor second choice. You can also explain to the undecided employer that you have another job offer but would prefer working with them and request that they let you know their decision as soon as possible. Here, too, be careful of your presentation. An employer's individual time constraints may still result in your having to make a decision on the first position without knowing about the second.

When you are in the fortunate position of having more than one job offer and must reject all but one offer, use the same tact and finesse that you would want from the employer. Carefully prepare what you will say, and be gracious. You never know what the future will bring. Someday you may have the opportunity (and desire) to work for that employer. Also, people you met with in an interview may be future networking contacts.

Closing Thoughts

There is no doubt that the practice of health law—in whatever practice setting or area of focus—is one of the most enjoyable fields of legal practice available to any attorney. The field is consequential, cutting edge, and staffed by some of the smartest and nicest people in the United States. As any health lawyer will tell you, the work is never boring.

The sheer breadth of the law and industry knowledge necessary to be a successful health lawyer can seem overwhelming at first. But remember, many before you had these same worries, and they succeeded in finding their niche. Health law is so dynamic and vibrant that no unique personality or single skill set is needed to succeed. If you devote hard work, curiosity, and passion to your education, job search, and career, we have no doubt that you too will find a "home" within the great field of health law.

Appendix A

Health Law and Bar Organizations

Here is a sampling of organizations you may wish to consider joining:

American Association of Legal Nurse Consultants, www.aalnc.org
American Association of Nurse Attorneys, www.taana.org
American Bar Association, Health Law Section, www.abanet.org/
health
American College of Healthcare Executives, www.ache.org
American College of Legal Medicine, www.aclm.org
American Health Lawyers Association, www.ahla.org
American Public Health Association, www.apha.org
American Society for Healthcare Risk Management, www.ashrm.org
American Society of Law, Medicine and Ethics, www.aslme.org
Food and Drug Law Institute, www.fdli.org
Healthcare Leadership Council, www.hlc.org
National Business Coalition on Health, www.nbch.org
National Health Care Anti-Fraud Association, www.nhcaa.org
National Society of Certified Healthcare Business Consultants,
http://www.nschbc.org/

Note: Many state and local bar associations also have sections devoted to
health law.

Appendix B

Federal Government Agency Websites

Federal Trade Commission, www.ftc.gov
Internal Revenue Service, www.irs.gov
Office of Diversion Control, www.deadiversion.usdoj.gov
U.S. Department of Health and Human Services, www.hhs.gov
   Agency for Healthcare Research and Quality, www.ahrq.gov
   Centers for Disease Control and Prevention, www.cdc.gov
   Centers for Medicare and Medicaid Services, www.cms.gov
   Food and Drug Administration, www.fda.gov
   Office of Inspector General, oig.hhs.gov
U.S. Department of Justice, Office of the United States Attorney, www.justice.gov
   Antitrust Division, www.justice.gov/atr
   Civil Division, www.justice.gov/civil
   Criminal Division, www.justice.gov/criminal
U.S. Department of Labor, www.dol.gov
U.S. Social Security Administration, www.ssa.gov

Searching for Jobs in the U.S. Government

To search for health law positions with the U.S. government, use the following websites:

Federal Jobs Digest, http://www.jobsfed.com
FedWorld.Gov, http://fedworld.ntis.gov
Go Government, http://gogovernment.org
GovtJobs.com, http://www.govtjobs.com
USAJOBS, https://www.usajobs.gov

Appendix C

Other Employers

Health Care Providers

Significant corporate, regulatory, transactional, patient care, reimbursement, labor, and other legal matters are addressed by in-house counsel working in our nation's hospitals, long-term care facilities, and other patient care facilities. To locate health care providers in the United States, see http://www.hospitalconnectsearch.com

Suppliers and Vendors

Companies that provide medical, surgical, and pharmaceutical products and services to health care providers have specific legal needs relating to the health care industry as well. There are many of these companies; here are some typical examples:

AIM Specialty Health, http://www.aimspecialtyhealth.com
Apria Healthcare, http://www.apria.com
Baxter, http://www.baxter.com
CVS Caremark Inc., https://www.caremark.com

Pharmaceutical and Medical Device Companies

Drug and medical device companies, like the following, discover new medicines and technologies for health promotion and disease prevention. Their products range from nutritional items and pharmaceutical therapies to medical devices and laboratory diagnostics. A sampling of leading firms include:

Abbott Laboratories, http://www.abbott.com
Boston Scientific, http://www.bostonscientific.com
Bristol-Myers Squibb, http://www.bms.com
Johnson and Johnson, http://www.jnj.com
Medtronic, http://www.medtronic.com
Novartis, http://www.novartis.com
Pfizer, http://www.pfizer.com

Public Interest Law

Many public interest law organizations offer opportunities to represent underserved populations in areas relating to health law, including disability discrimination and benefits, Medicare and Medicaid coverage, government benefits and insurance, elder law, and others. Examples of public interest organizations working in areas related to health law include:

Access Living, http://www.accessliving.org
Equip for Equality, http://www.equipforequality.org
Health and Disability Advocates, http://www.hdadvocates.org
Legal Assistance Foundation of Metropolitan Chicago,
http://www.lafchicago.org

Health Care Trade Associations

Health care trade associations represent, and serve as advocates and leaders for, their respective member organizations. Trade associations and professional organizations require a broad range of legal counsel and services, including regulatory, tort reform, and contract issues, including work in the legislative, executive, and administrative arenas. Some examples include:

American College of Health Care Administrators, http://www.achca.org
American College of Legal Medicine, http://www.aclm.org
American Dental Association, http://www.ada.org
American Health Care Association, http://www.ahcancal.org
American Health Information Management Association, http://www.ahima.org
American Hospital Association, http://www.aha.org
American Medical Association, http://www.ama-assn.org
American Pharmacists Association, http://www.pharmacist.com
American Society of Health-System Pharmacists, http://www.ashp.org
Health Care Compliance Association, https://www.hcca-info.org
Healthcare Billing and Management Association, http://www.hbma.org
Healthcare Financial Management Association, http://www.hfma.org
The Joint Commission, http://www.jointcommission.org

Insurers and Payors

Health insurance companies of all types hire lawyers to work on corporate, contractual, regulatory, reimbursement, and litigation matters. Some examples of large health insurance companies include:

Aetna, http://www.aetna.com
Anthem BlueCross BlueShield, http://www.anthem.com
BlueCross BlueShield of Illinois, http://www.bcbsil.com
CareFirst, https://www.carefirst.com
Humana, https://www.humana.com
UniCare, https://www.unicare.com
United Healthcare, http://www.uhc.com

Consulting Firms

Consulting firms assist academic medical centers, private medical practices, hospitals, ambulatory businesses, and other health care providers in improving their structure, efficiency, and financial bottom line. Health care consulting firms prefer to hire individuals with directly related, relevant health care experience as well as business experience. Some examples of consulting firms that have health care practices include:

Capgemini, http://www.capgemini.com
Ernst & Young, http://www.ey.com
First Chesapeake Group, http://www.firstchesapeakegroup.com
Health Directions, http://www.healthdirections.com
The Health Law Consultancy, http://hlconsultancy.com/
Healthcare Strategies, http://www.hcare.net/hcs/home.html
Huron Consulting Group, http://www.huronconsultinggroup.com
KPMG, http://www.kpmg.com
Lewin Group, http://www.lewin.com
Mercer, http://www.mercer.com
Murer Consulting, http://www.murer.com
Navigant Consulting, http://www.navigant.com
PricewaterhouseCoopers, http://www.pwc.com
Research and Planning Consultants, http://www.rpcconsulting.com
The Stein Consultancy, http://www.thesteinconsultancy.com
Towers Watson, http://www.towerswatson.com

Appendix D

Health Care Publications

A sampling of leading health care-related publications includes the following:

ACHE Newsletter
Catholic Health World
Chicago Hospital News
Compliance Today
Compliance Week
Crain's Chicago Business—Chicago Healthcare Daily
Fierce Healthcare Newsletter
Health Care Finance News
The Health Lawyer
Healthcare Business Monthly
Healthcare Executive Magazine
Healthcare Financial Management Association Magazine
Healthcare Times
Hospitals & Health Networks Magazine
Modern Healthcare

Appendix E

Health Law Writing Competitions

A sampling of writing competitions in health law includes the following. It is recommended that entrants carefully check each competition's specific rules and regulations. The following information is intended as a general guide only.

ABA Commission on Mental and Physical Disability Law Adam A. Milani Disability Law Writing Competition
- Early June deadline
- Requires an appellate brief, up to 20 pages double-spaced
- Prizes range from $300 to $1,000

ABA Gellhorn-Sargentich Law Student Writing Competition (Regulatory and Administrative Law)
- Early May deadline
- Requires up to 40 pages double-spaced
- Prize is $5,000 plus airfare to section's fall conference; includes publication opportunity

ABA Health Law Section Annual Health Law Student Writing Competition
- Early December deadline
- Requires 20–25 pages, double-spaced (minimum 5,000 words)
- Prize is $500, publication in *The Health Lawyer*, and airfare and per diem to attend the ABA's Conference on Emerging Issues in Healthcare Law

American College of Legal Medicine Student Writing
Competition in Law, Medicine & Bioethics

- Early January deadline
- Requires no more than 5,000 words or 15 pages double-spaced
- Prizes range from $250 to $1,000 and include travel and lodging to present at the organization's annual meeting

Center for Alcohol Policy

- Early December deadline
- Requires no more than 25 pages double-spaced
- Prizes range from $1,000 to $5,000

Epstein Becker Green Health Law Writing Competition

- Late January deadline
- Requires 30 pages or less, double-spaced
- Prizes range from $500 to $4,000 and include possible publication in the *Annals of Health Law*

Florida State University Mollie and Paul Hill Student Writing
Competition in Medical-Legal Interprofessional Collaboration

- Early January deadline
- Requires 1,200–5,000 words
- Prize is $250

Food and Drug Law Institute H. Thomas Austern Memorial Writing Competition

- Early June deadline
- One competition for papers up to 40 pages, one for 40–100 pages (double-spaced)
- Prizes range from $1,000 to $4,000

Law Students for Reproductive Justice Sarah Weddington Prize
for Student Scholarship in Reproductive Rights Law

- Early January deadline
- Requires minimum of 20 pages double-spaced

- Prizes range from $250 to $750 and include opportunity to publish in *NYU Review of Law and Social Change*

Richard D. Cudahy Writing Competition on Regulatory and Administrative Law
- Early February deadline
- Requires under 25,000 words
- Prize is $1,500

Résumé and Cover Letter Examples

The following sample resumes and cover letters are intended to provide examples of how applicants may emphasize their health law interest and experience when applying for jobs in the field.

Jane Smith

Student@email.edu • 100 North Avenue, Atlanta, GA • (555) 555-5555

EDUCATION

Jurisprudence School of Law, Baltimore, MD
Juris Doctor, anticipated May 2014
GPA: 3.4/4.0   Rank: X/238, Top _%; Dean's List: Fall 2012, Spring 2013
Honors: CALI Awards for highest grade in Property Law
            Honors-At-Entrance Scholarship
Activities: Academic Tutor, Property Law; Health Law Society, Member
Publication: *Health Law*, 16 LOY. U. CHI. L.J. 22 (2012).

Undergraduate University, Boston, MA
Bachelor of Arts in Political Science, Minor in Economics, May 2009
GPA: 3.5/4.0   Dean's List: 2008, 2009
Activities: Varsity Field Hockey Team, Captain, 2005 – 2008, (NCAA Finalist 2008); New England Small College
            Athletic Conference (NESCAC) *All-Sportsmanship Award* 2008
Study Abroad: **North State University**, Madrid, Spain, Spring 2008

PROFESSIONAL EXPERIENCE

Big Firm, Washington, D.C.
Summer Associate, May 2013 - Present
- Research and draft memoranda regarding various Medicare and Affordable Care Act regulations promulgated by the Centers for Medicare and Medicaid Services, state physician licensure laws, and applicability of Medicare guaranteed renewability to health insurance plans
- Prepare checklist of action items for entities to comply with HIPAA Omnibus Rule; assist in filing Medicaid and Medicare reimbursement appeals on behalf of hospitals

Legal Aid Organization, Chicago, IL
Legal Volunteer, Spring 2013 - Present
- Interview and assist individuals seeking to expunge their criminal records

Physician Advocacy Association, State Center, Chicago, IL
Legal Extern, Summer 2012
- Researched and prepared 50-state survey on standardization of prior authorization forms

United States District Court for the Western District of State, Seattle, WA
Judicial Intern for Magistrate Judge Abraham Lincoln, Summer 2012
- Drafted opinions in cases regarding Social Security Disability Insurance claims, contract law, and trademark law

Large Firm, Chicago, IL
Litigation Case Assistant, June 2009 - June 2011
- Led complex business litigation, off-label marketing and anti-kickback government investigation, and antitrust case teams in document production; reviewed documents for case analysis and factual development
- Drafted, filed, and served court motions and discovery notices
- Created, implemented and managed organizational systems for files and case teams

Insurance and Financial Services Company, Boston, MA
Research Assistant, May 2008 - August 2008
- Assisted Compliance Department in preparation of documents in state-by-state regulatory project

John Smith

Attorney@email.com • 100 North Avenue, Chicago, IL • (555) 555-5555

EDUCATION

JURISPRUDENCE SCHOOL OF LAW, Durham, NC
Juris Doctor, *cum laude*, Certificate in Health Law, January 2013, GPA: 3.3/4.000
Honors: Health Law Fellow
                Health Law Journal, Editorial Board Member
                Texas Invitational Moot Court Team (2012) and City Bar Association Moot Court Team (2010)
UNDERGRADUATE UNIVERSITY, Milwaukee, WI
Bachelor of Arts in Public Relations and Political Science, *cum laude*, May 2006
Center for Government, Washington, DC, August 2005-December 2005

EXPERIENCE

BIG FIRM, Los Angeles, CA
Associate Attorney, June 2013-Present
- Draft contracts on behalf of health systems, hospitals, physicians and federally qualified health centers
- Advise clients on Medicare and Medicaid compliance issues including self-disclosures
- Assist healthcare facilities with Medicare and Medicaid applications and federal tax exemption applications

NON-PROFIT ORGANIZATION, Washington, DC and Chicago, IL
Associate Director, Youth Advocacy, March 2007-January 2012
- Planned and executed nationwide youth advocacy and media initiatives to achieve state and federal legislative goals
- Organized Kick Butts Day, a national day of youth advocacy generating over 30 million media impressions
- Oversaw the Youth Advocate of the Year program including the development of application materials and the selection process of award winners
- Managed all contracts and budgets for national youth advocacy initiatives, and secured sustainable grant funding

COMMUNICATIONS FIRM, Chicago, IL
Assistant Account Executive, June 2006-March 2007
- Drafted media materials and completed daily monitoring for Consumer Healthcare Publication
- Researched validity of facts, background information on spokespeople, and copyrights/trademarks

INTERNSHIPS

MIDSIZE FIRM, Milwaukee, WI
Law Clerk, May 2012-August 2012
HONORABLE JUDGE, PRESIDING MAGISTRATE JUDGE FOR THE N.D. OF STATE, Los Angeles, CA
Judicial Extern, September 2011-December 2011
STATE OFFICE OF HEALTH INFORMATION TECHNOLOGY, Seattle, WA
Legal Task Force Intern, November 2010-August 2011
GOVERNMENT FOUNDATION, Washington, DC
Government Relations Intern, September 2005-December 2005
FEDERAL COMMISSION, Washington, DC
Bureau of Protection Intern, September 2005-December 2005

PUBLICATIONS

- John Smith, *Health Law*, 5 ANNALS HEALTH L. J. 2, 2013.
- Centers for Government Health, *Health Law Best Practices*. Atlanta: U.S. Department of Health and Human Services, Office on Health, 2010.

Jean Smith

123 Alphabet Lane, 6B, Seattle, Washington 12345
attorney@email.com, (555) 555-5555

November 1, 20XX

Large Hospital
Office of the General Counsel
Attorney at Law, Associate General Counsel
321 W. North St.
Los Angeles, CA 54321

Dear Ms. At Law:

I am writing to express my interest in working for you as a student extern during the upcoming spring semester. Currently, I am a student in the Jurisprudence Law School LLM program. I would like to offer my services beginning in January and will have a flexible schedule (I will be available Monday through Wednesday from 9am - 4pm and all day on Fridays).

Unlike most of my fellow LLM students, I began the program after five years of experience as a transactional attorney for Medium Firm. After much consideration, I decided to leave the firm to refocus my career on health care regulation and compliance. I am especially interested in the unique regulatory challenges faced by a leading academic medical center such as Large Hospital, and I know that the practical experience offered by the externship will be invaluable in refocusing my career.

My professional experience, commitment to the health care field and continued studies have armed me with the tools necessary to be not only an enthusiastic extern, but also a valuable and productive extern. In particular, my time at Medium Firm honed my attention to detail, sharpened my research skills and made me particularly effective at expressing thought in both speech and writing. In addition, the seriousness of purpose that comes with a career change allows me to assure you of my dedication.

I have attached my resume and I would welcome the chance to speak with you. Thank you for your consideration.

Sincerely,

Jean Smith

Jack Smith

123 Alphabet Lane, 6B, Chicago, Illinois 12345
attorney@email.com, (555) 555-5555

January 1, 20XX

Ms. At Law
Attorney Recruiting and Development Manager
Large Law Firm
1 North Street
Washington, DC 20036

Dear Ms. At Law:

I am a second-year student at Jurisprudence School of Law, and I am writing to apply for a 2013 summer associate position with your firm. I am especially interested in working in your health law practice in Washington, D.C. I would welcome the opportunity to return to my hometown to work at Large Law Firm as a summer associate and explore the broad array of legal challenges facing the firm's clients.

In my first year at Jurisprudence, I established a record of academic achievement, ranking in the top X percent of my class. In the upcoming year, I will serve as a member of the *Jurisprudence Law Journal* and as an academic tutor for a first-year Property course.

Over the past year, I have worked to develop my knowledge and analytical skills in the health care field by enrolling in Introduction to Health Law as my elective course this past spring, and working at the American Medical Association this summer, where I researched and prepared a 50-state survey on the standardization of prior authorization forms. I also refined the research and writing skills I have developed in law school, and as a judicial extern for the Honorable Magistrate Judge John Smith of the District Court for the District of Illinois. Next year I will continue to pursue the Health Law Certificate by taking Health Care Corporate Transactions and other health law courses.

I am confident that my skills, qualifications, and experience make me a strong candidate for a summer associate position at your firm. My resume and transcript are attached for your review, and references are available upon request. Thank you for your time and consideration, and I look forward to hearing from you.

Sincerely,

Jack Smith

Index

consulting firms as, 69–70, 146

health law careers in, 31, 63–65,
    120–122, 143, 145

insurance or payor entities as,
    69–70, 145

lawyers transitioning to,
    120–122

pharmaceutical and medical
    device companies as,
    31, 63, 68–69, 144

providers as, 63, 64–65, 143

suppliers and vendors as, 63,
    68–69, 143–144

insurance industry

as law firm clients, 50–51

career profile in, 26–27

health care industry role of, 5

in-house counsel in, 69–70, 145

insurance law and, 25–26,
    59–60

Patient Protection and
    Affordable Care Act
    impacting, 27–28, 34,
    59

provider integration with, 25

regulation of, 27–28, 33–34, 59

Internal Revenue Service, U.S.
    (IRS), 56–57, 141

interviews

answering questions in,
    128–130

attire for, 127–128

behavioral, 132–134

discussing résumé in, 126,
    127–128

group/team, 133–134

health law market knowledge
    use during, 97

informational meetings as
    preparation for, 102

job offer acknowledgment after,
    134–135

job offer responses after,
    134–135

logistics of, 128–129

materials to bring to, 128

negative questions asked in, 130

nonverbal communication in,
    128–129

phone or Skype, 133–134

post-interview behavior, 134

preparation for, 126–127

questions asked of employer in,
    131–132

questions asked of interviewee
    in, 128–130

status monitoring after,
    134–135

thank you expressions after, 134

J

Joint Commission, The, 145

K

Kernek, Sterling, 65

L

labor and employment law, 29–30,
    56

law firms